# ATOMS, MOLECULES & QUANTUM MECHANICS FOR KIDS

**BABY PROFESSOR**
EDUCATION KIDS

Speedy Publishing LLC
40 E. Main St. #1156
Newark, DE 19711
www.speedypublishing.com

Copyright 2016

All Rights reserved. No part of this book may be reproduced or used in any way or form or by any means whether electronic or mechanical, this means that you cannot record or photocopy any material ideas or tips that are provided in this book

# PHYSICS

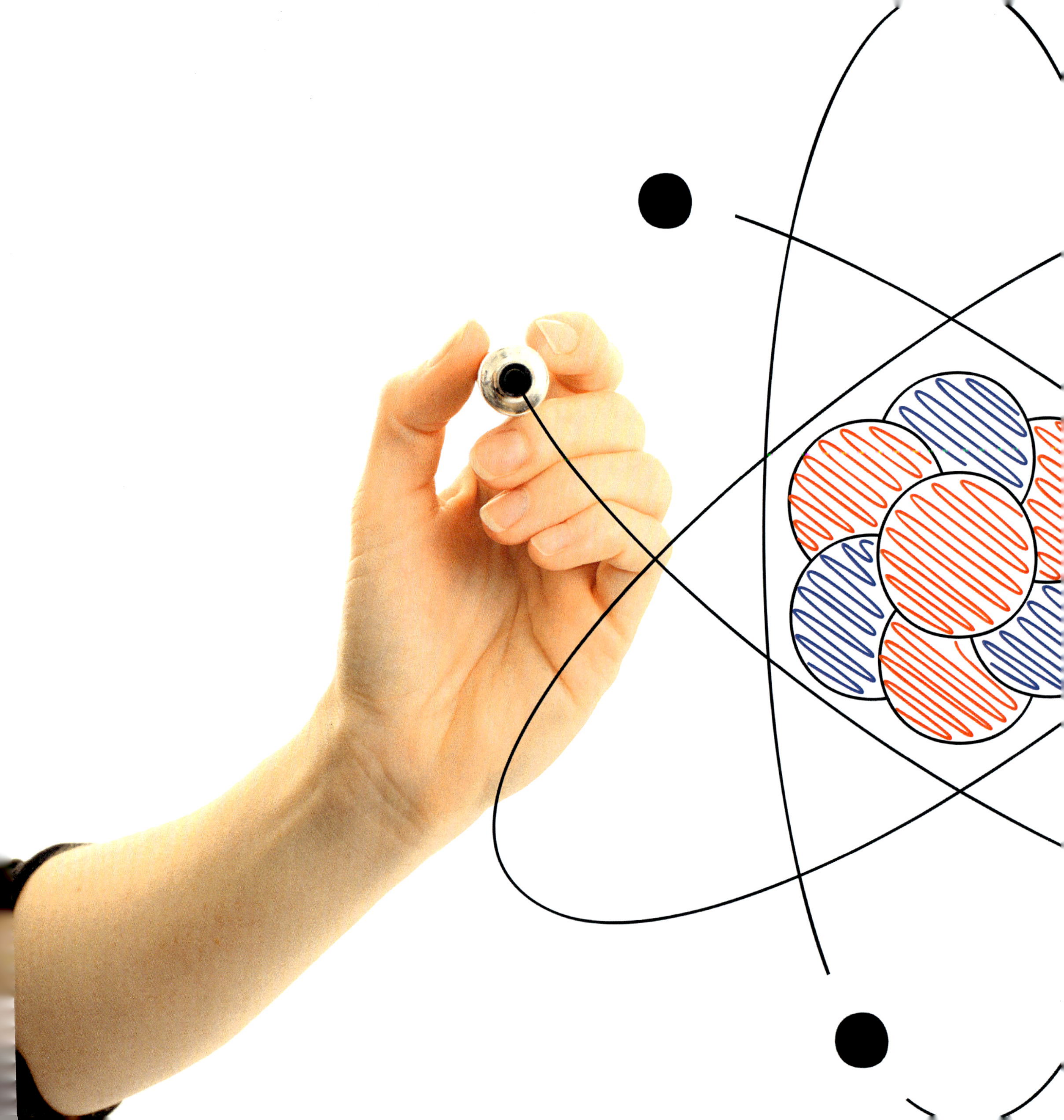

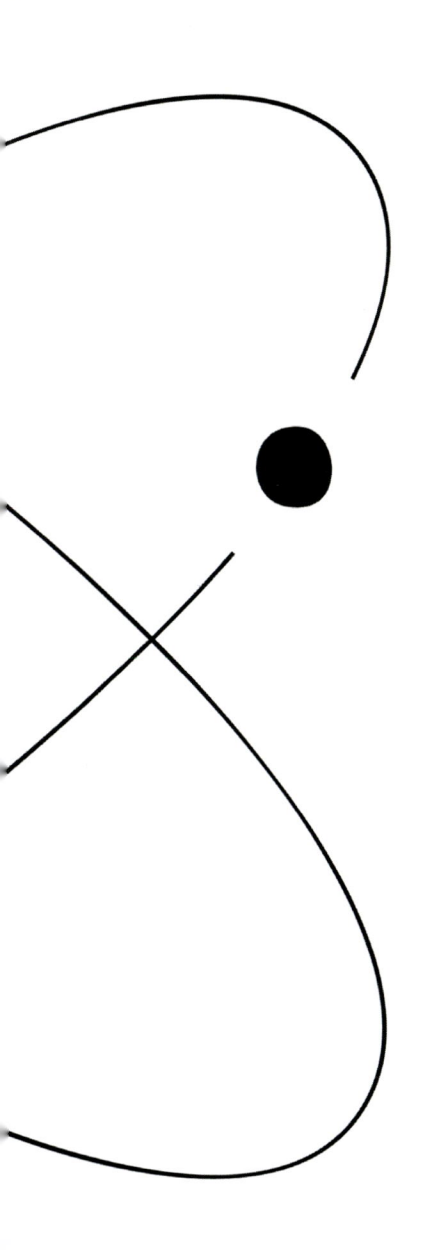

The atom is the foundation of chemistry. In fact, the atom is the basic building block for all matter in the universe.

Atoms are extremely tiny and are made up of a few even tinier particles. They are so small you can't see them, except through a special microscope. Atoms are collections of tiny bits of electrical energy.

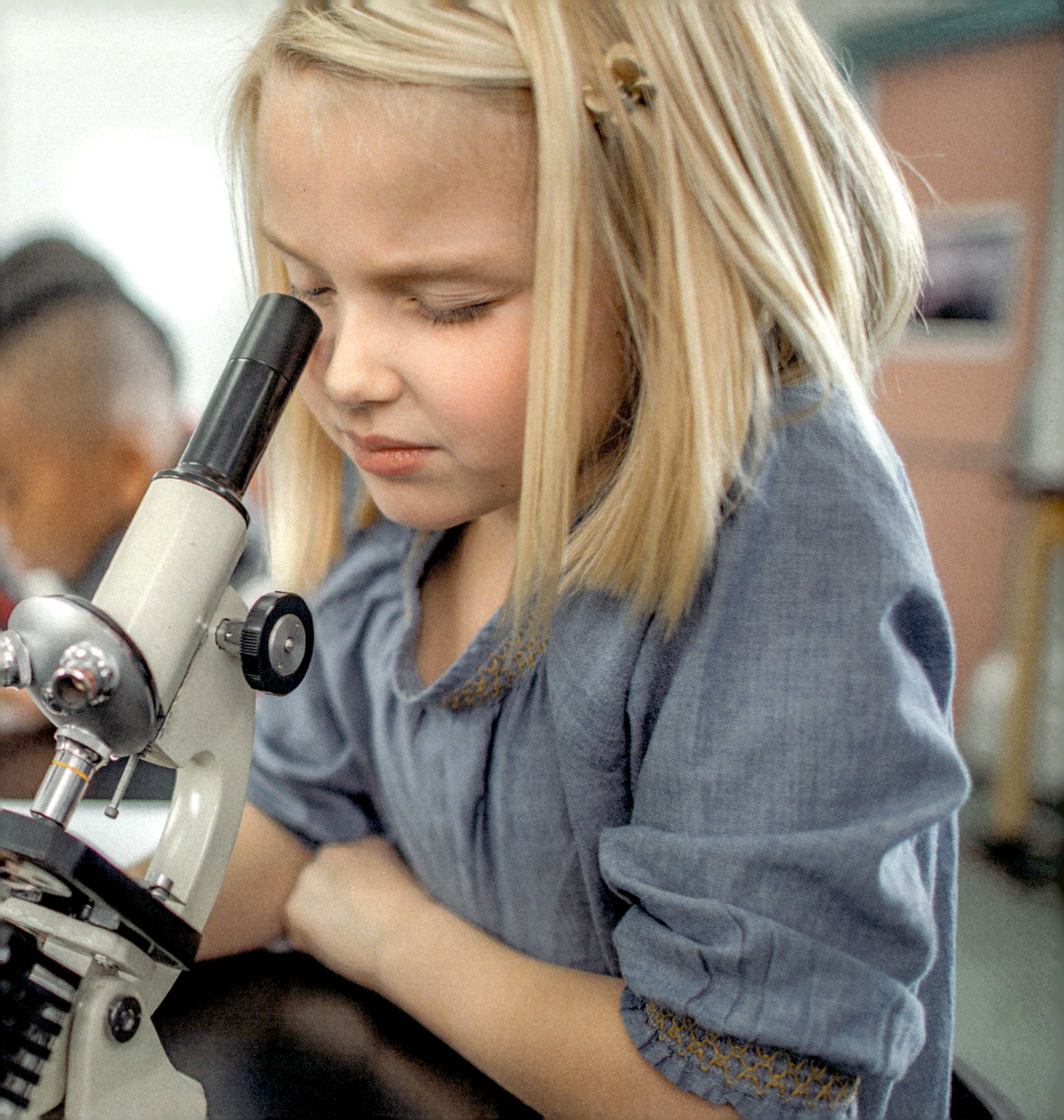

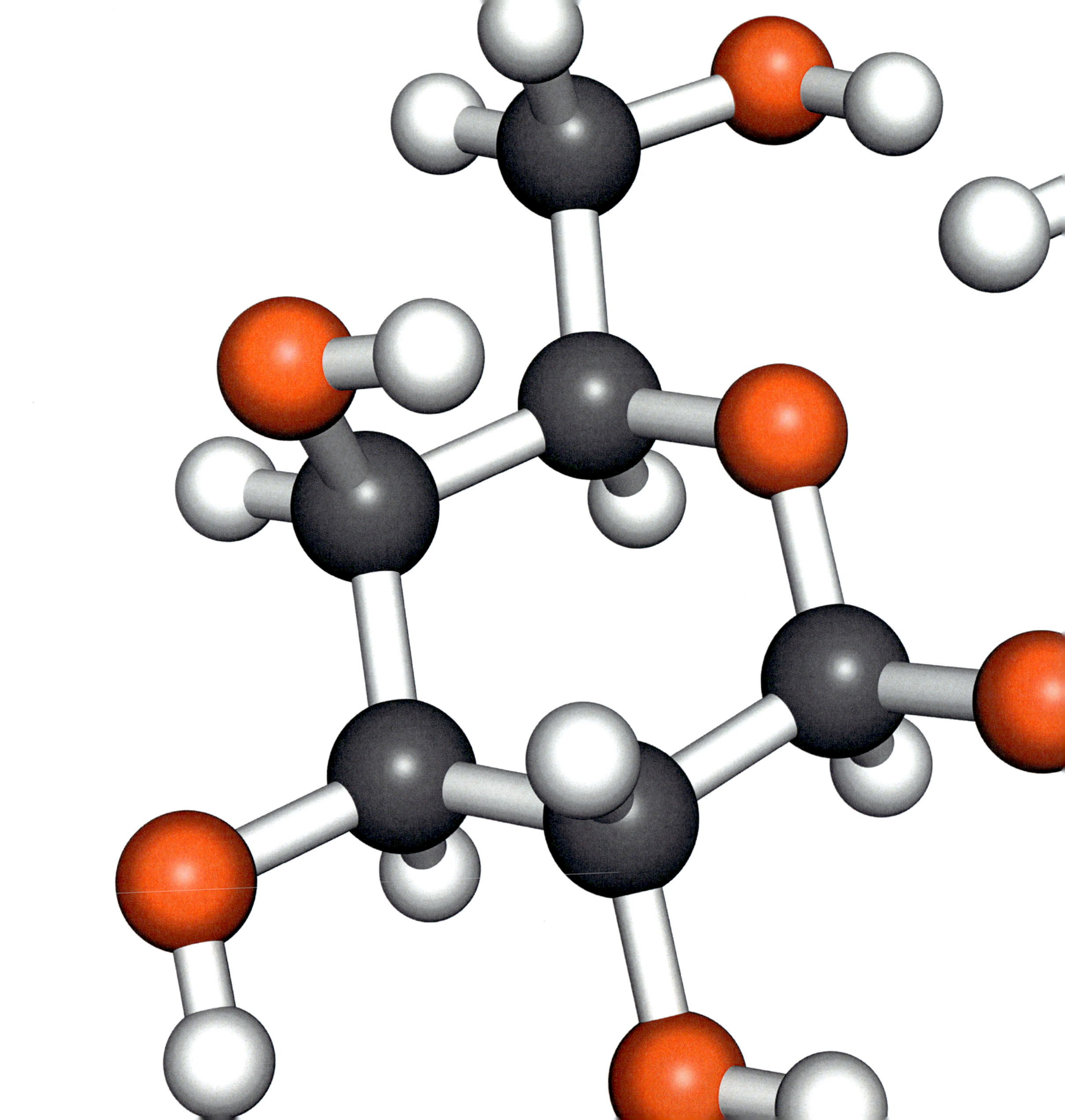

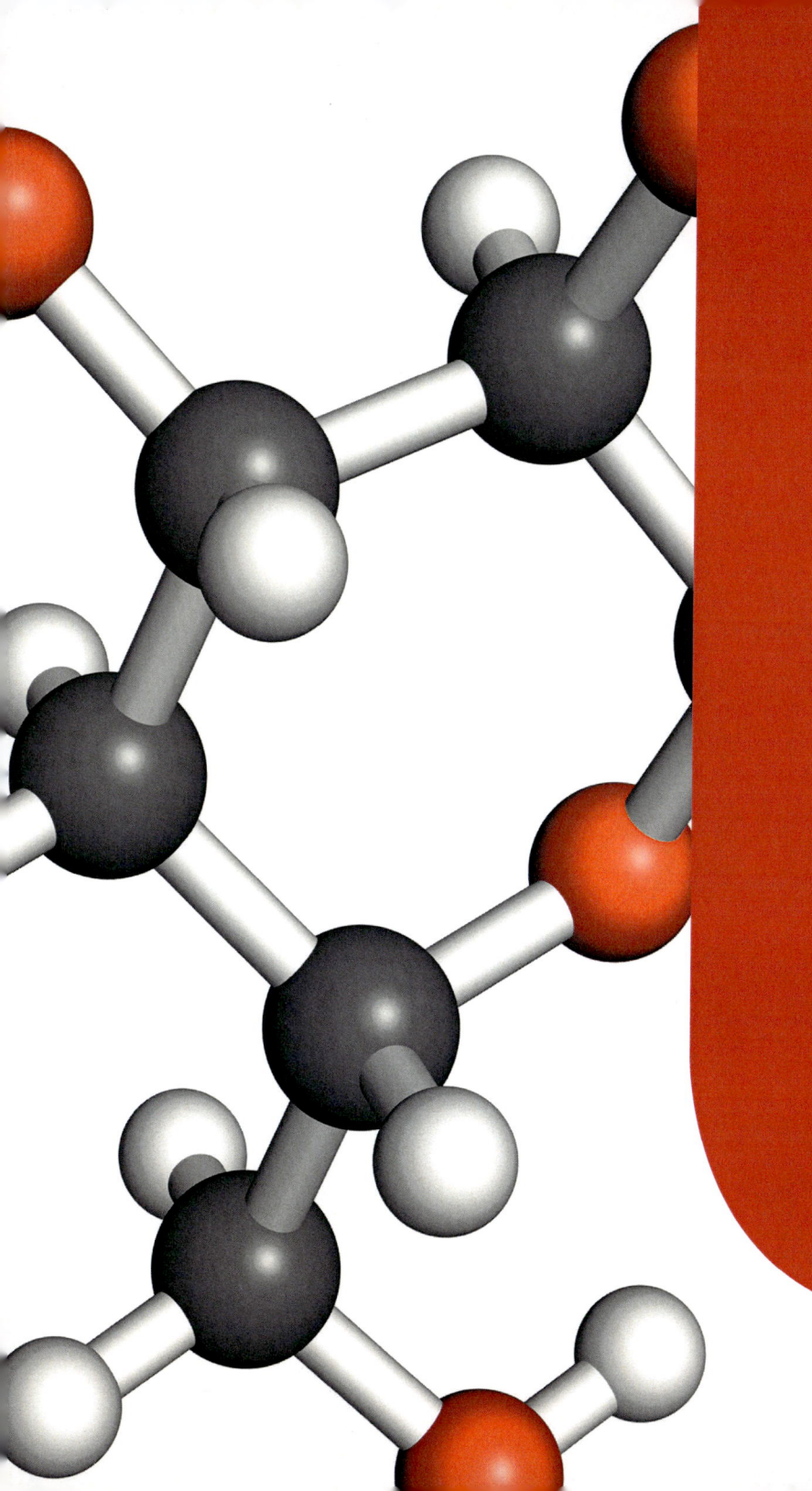

Atoms can last a long time, essentially forever. Atoms can transform and go through chemical reactions.

Matter is composed of atoms. When atoms fit together we can call that state "matter". Solids are made of atoms that are close to each other while gases have atoms that are spread out.

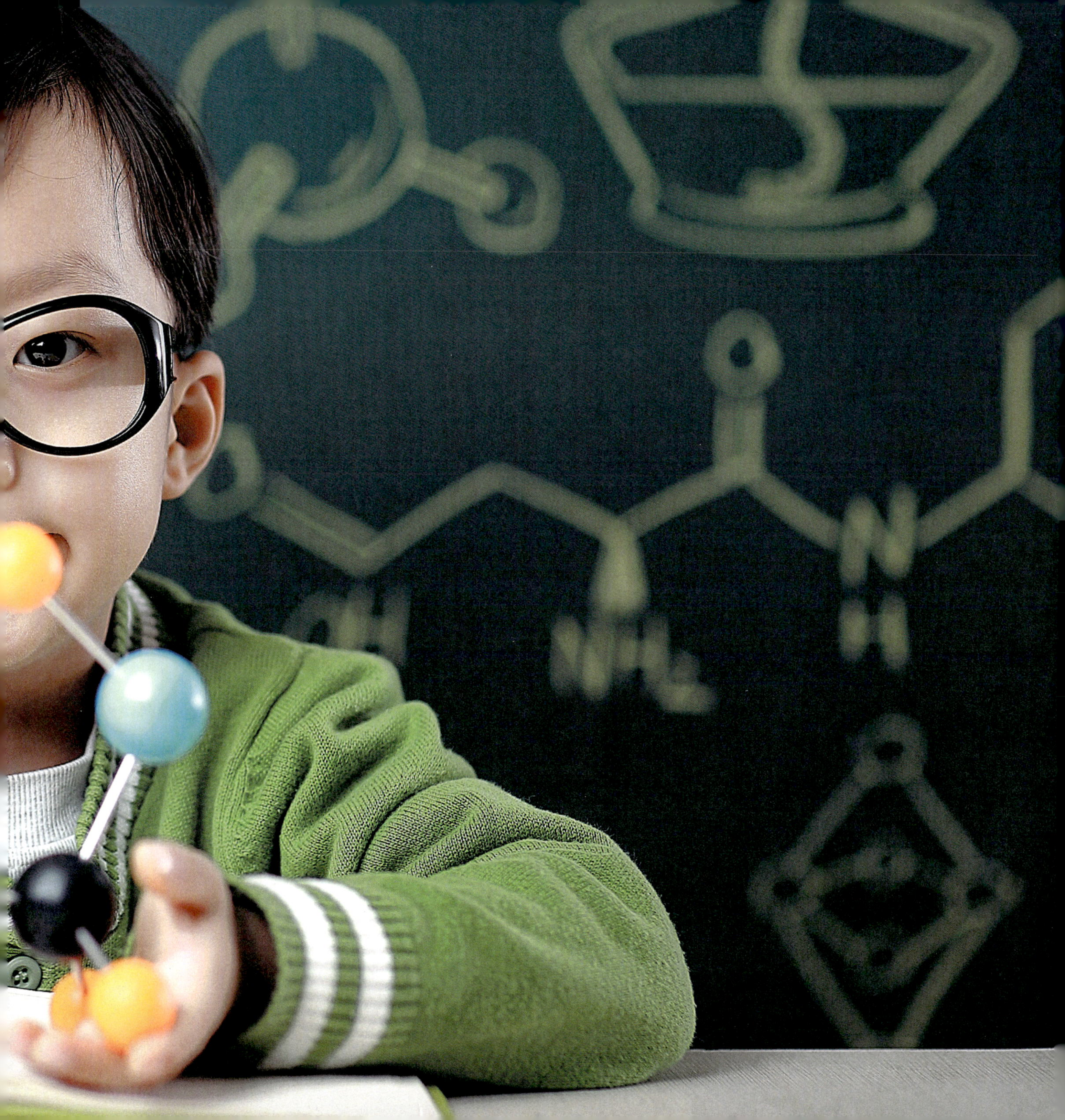

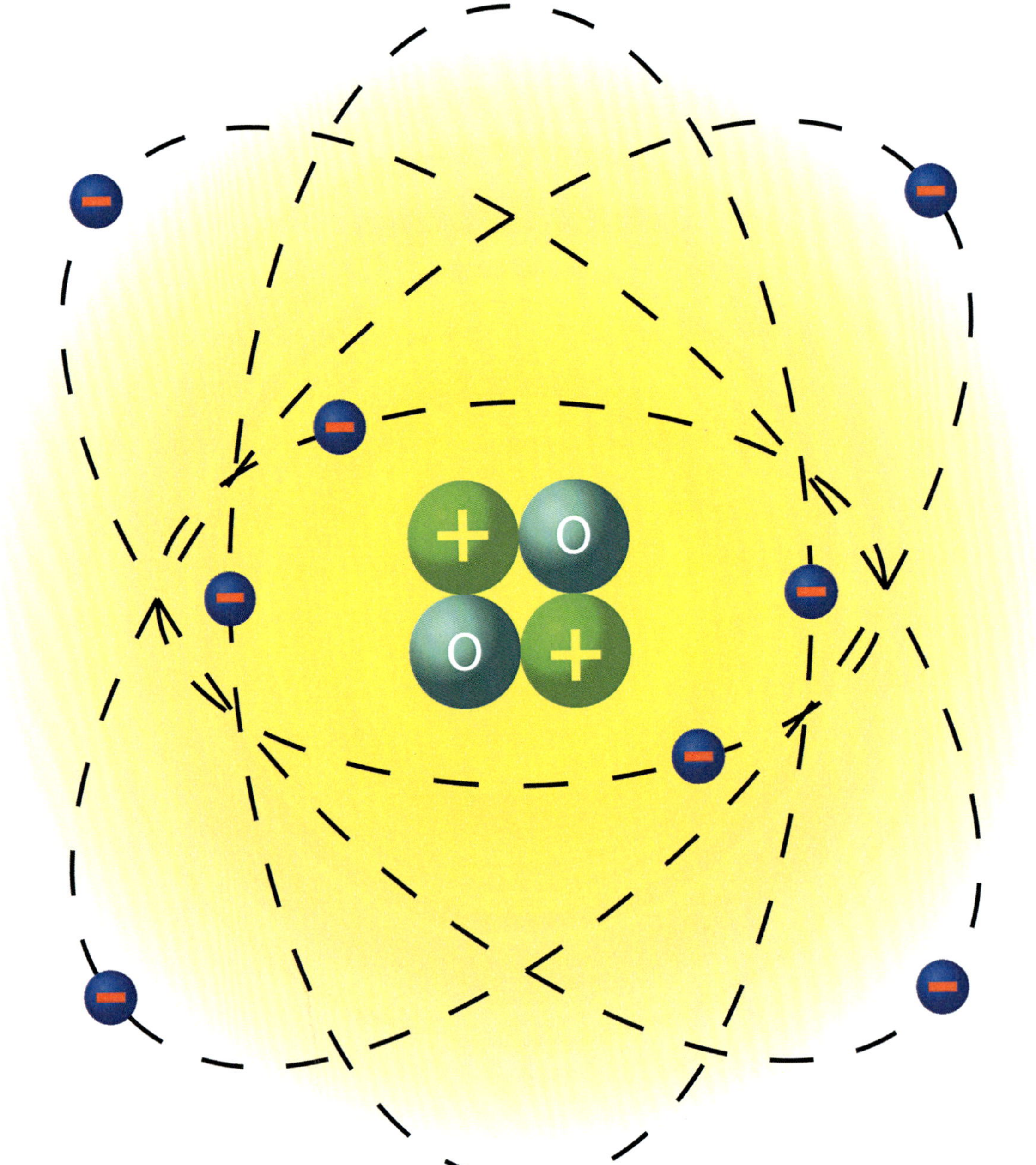

+ Proton

O Neutron

− Electron

Atoms have three basic parts. They are the electrons, protons, and neutrons. These are the basic particles that make up an atom.

Electrons, protons, and neutrons are found in the structure of the atom. The nucleus is at the center of the atom.

E for ELECTRON

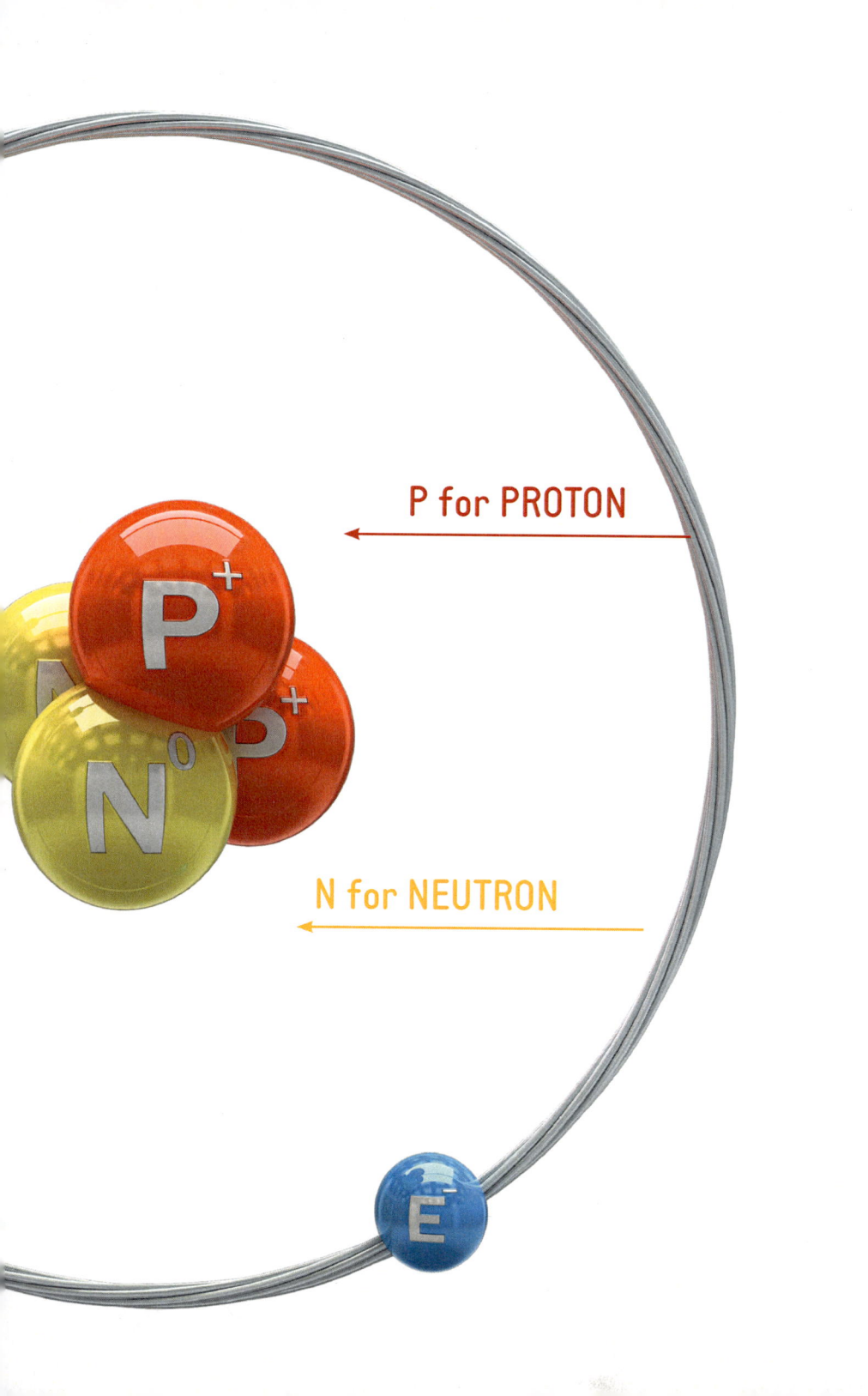

P for PROTON

N for NEUTRON

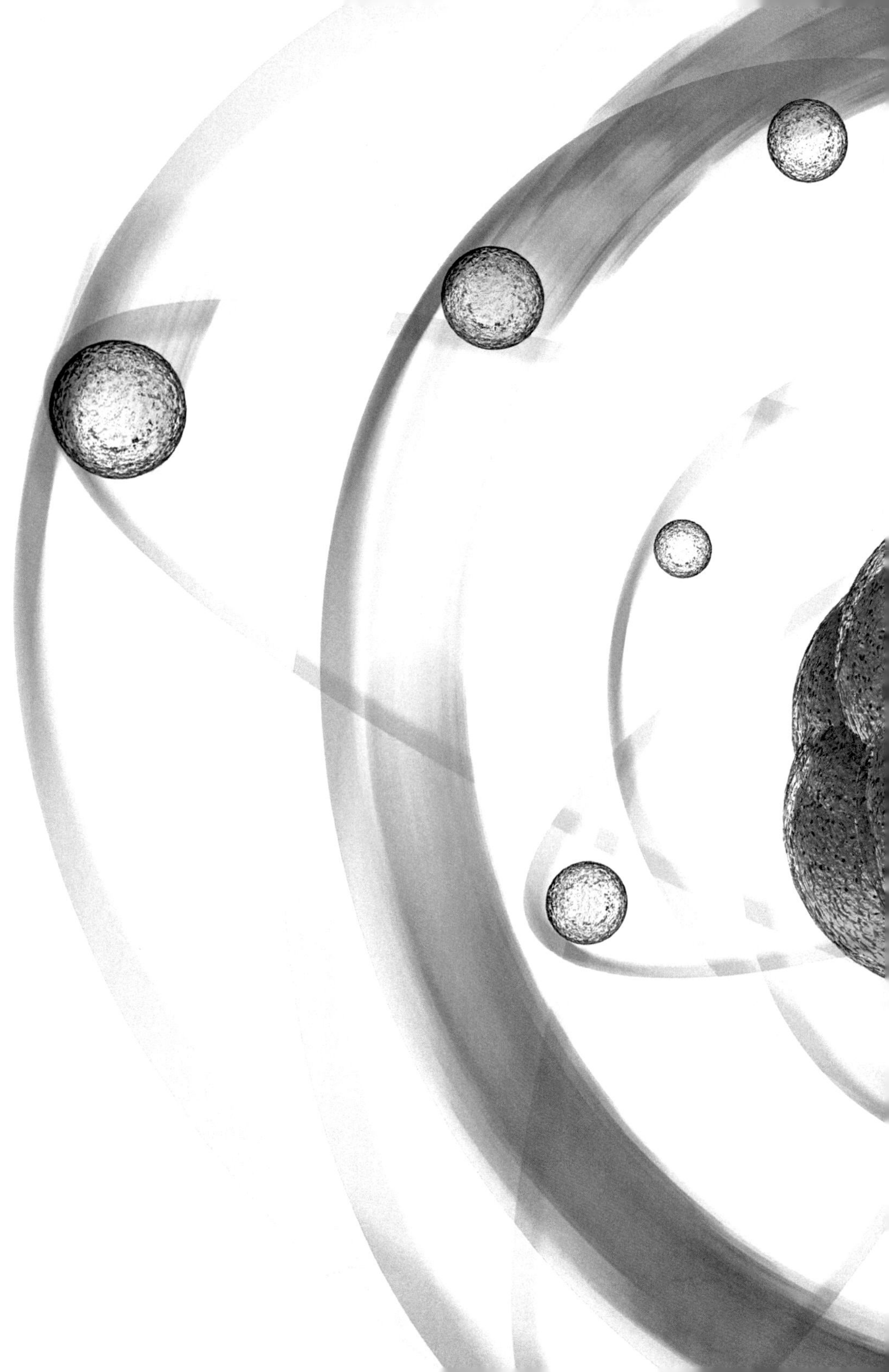

The nucleus is made up of protons and neutrons while the electrons orbit around the nucleus. But is it is not like the way the moon orbits the Earth.

The protons and neutrons group together inside the nucleus. Electrons are the tiniest of the three particles. Electrons are found in shells, sometimes called energy levels.

P for PROTON

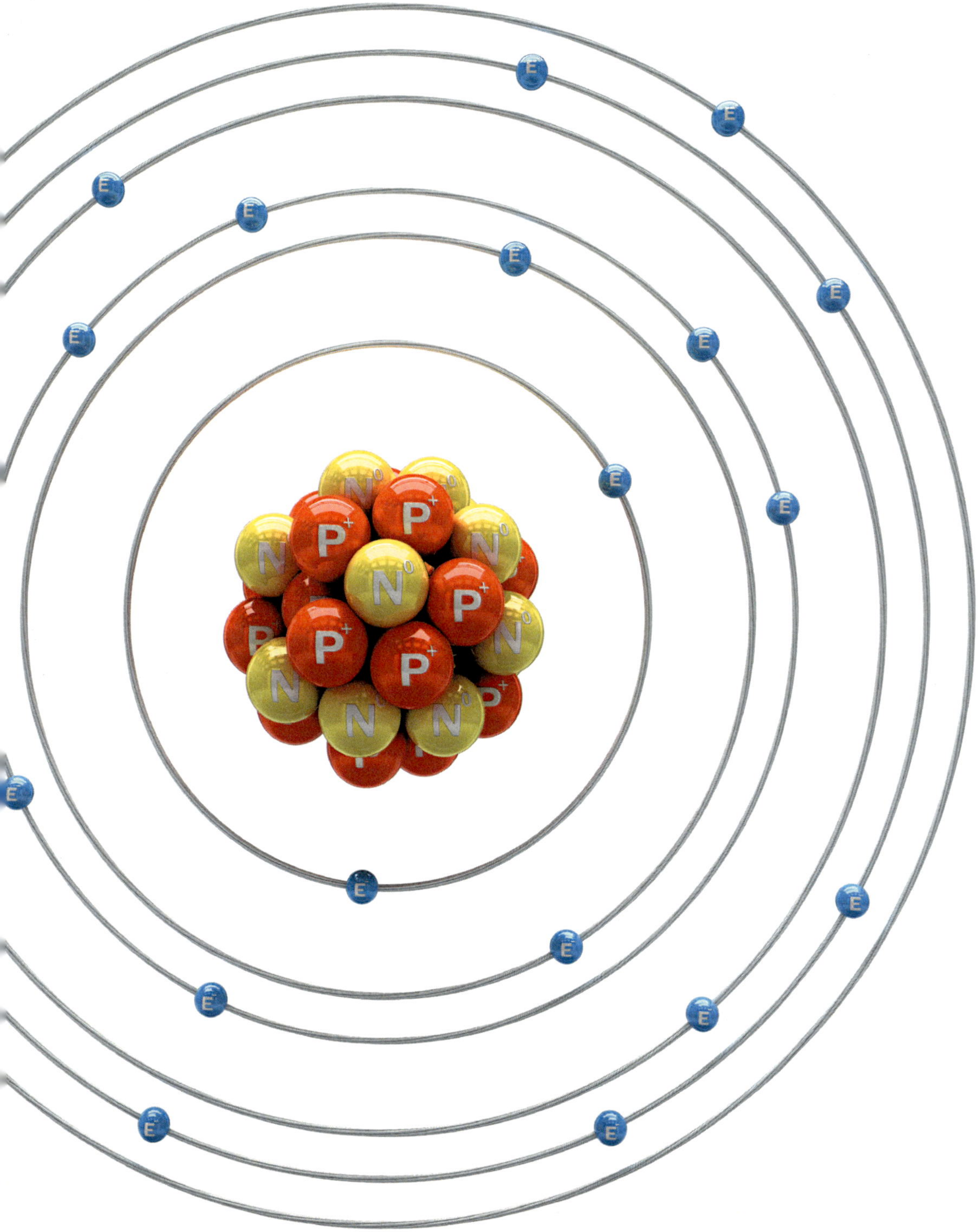

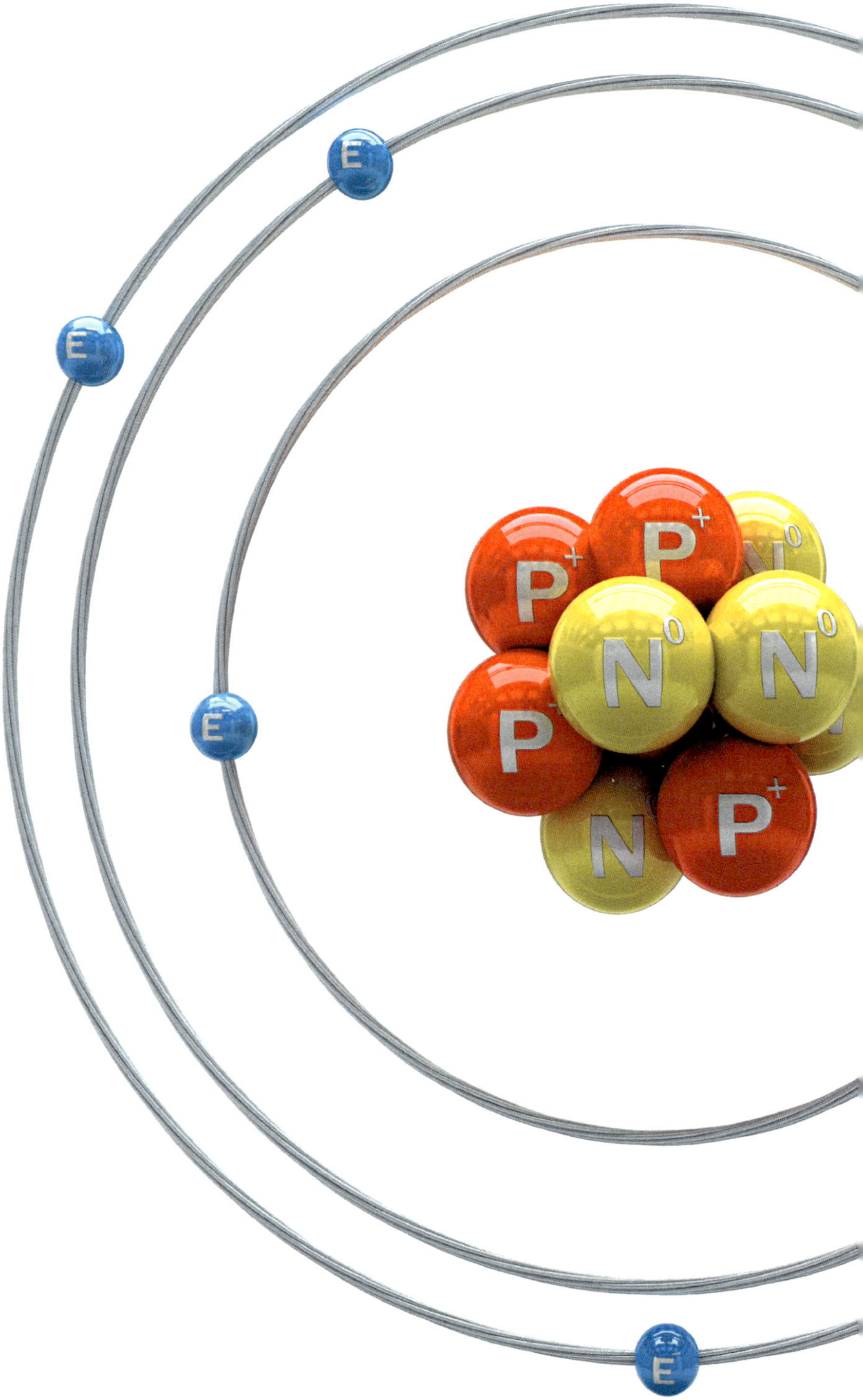

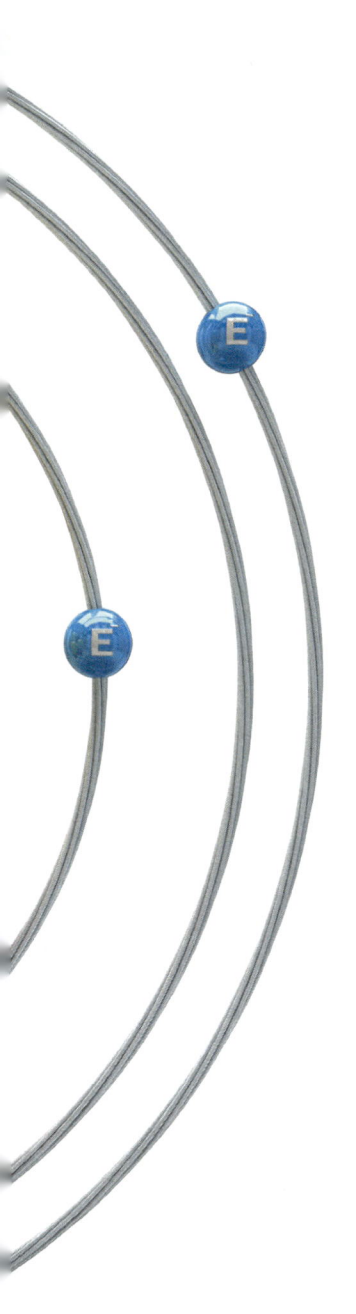

The proton is a positively charged particle. It is just about 2000 times more massive than an electron. Protons push away from each other because they have positive electrical charge.

The electron is a negatively charged particle. It orbits the nucleus of the atom and spins very fast around the nucleus. Electrons are smaller than neutrons and protons.

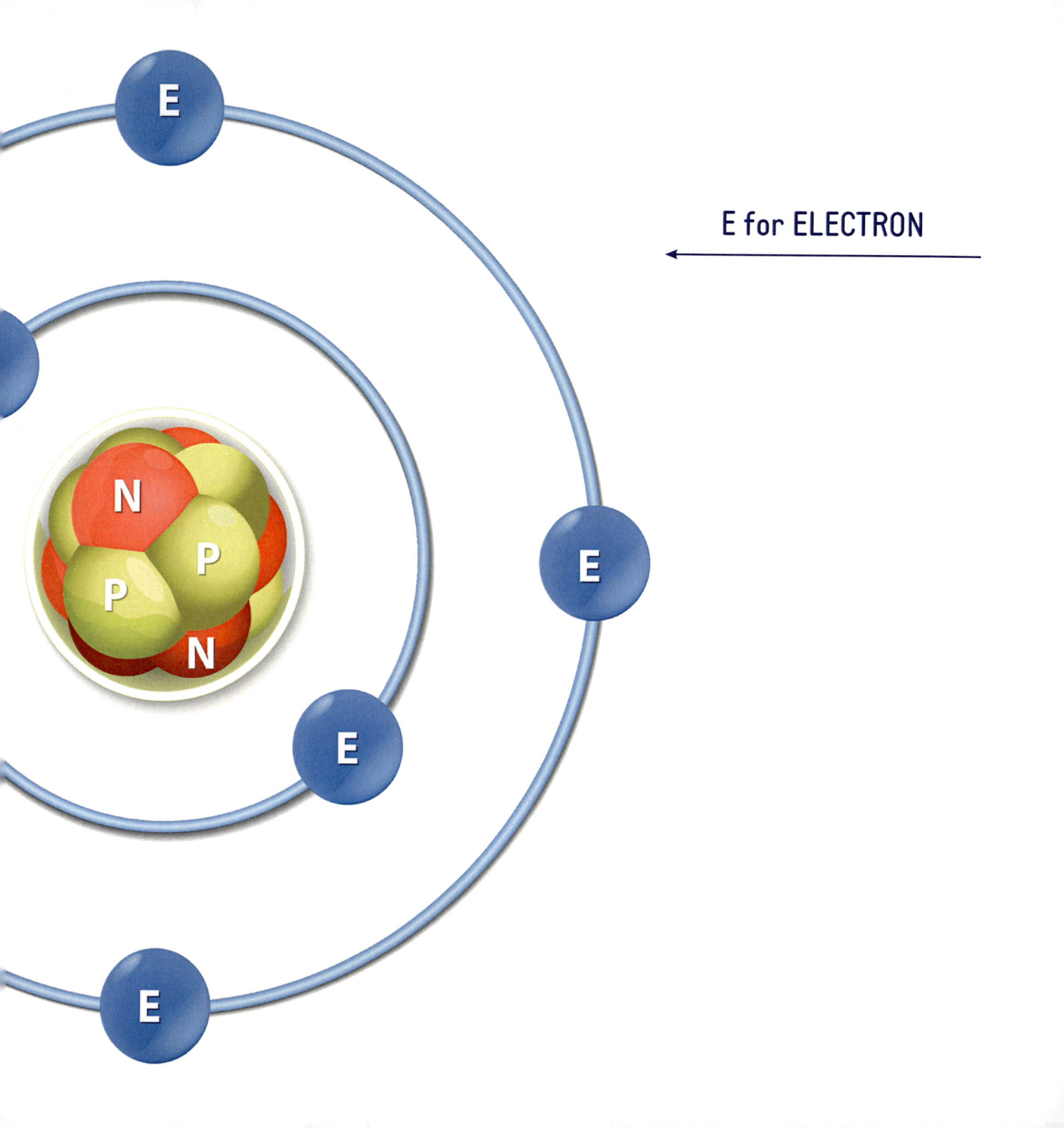

E for ELECTRON

N for NEUTRON

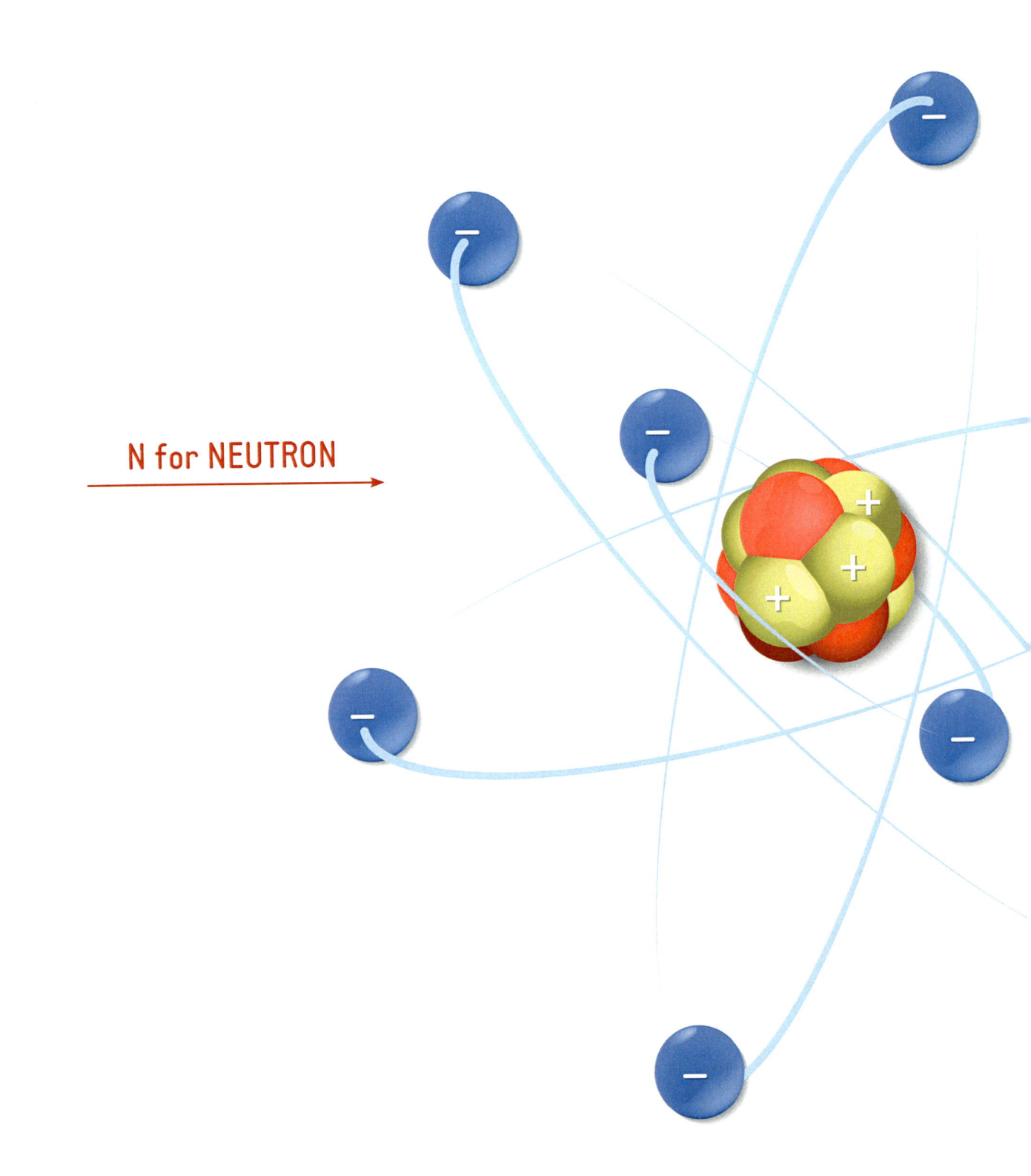

The neutron doesn't have any electrical charge. It weighs just the same as a proton.

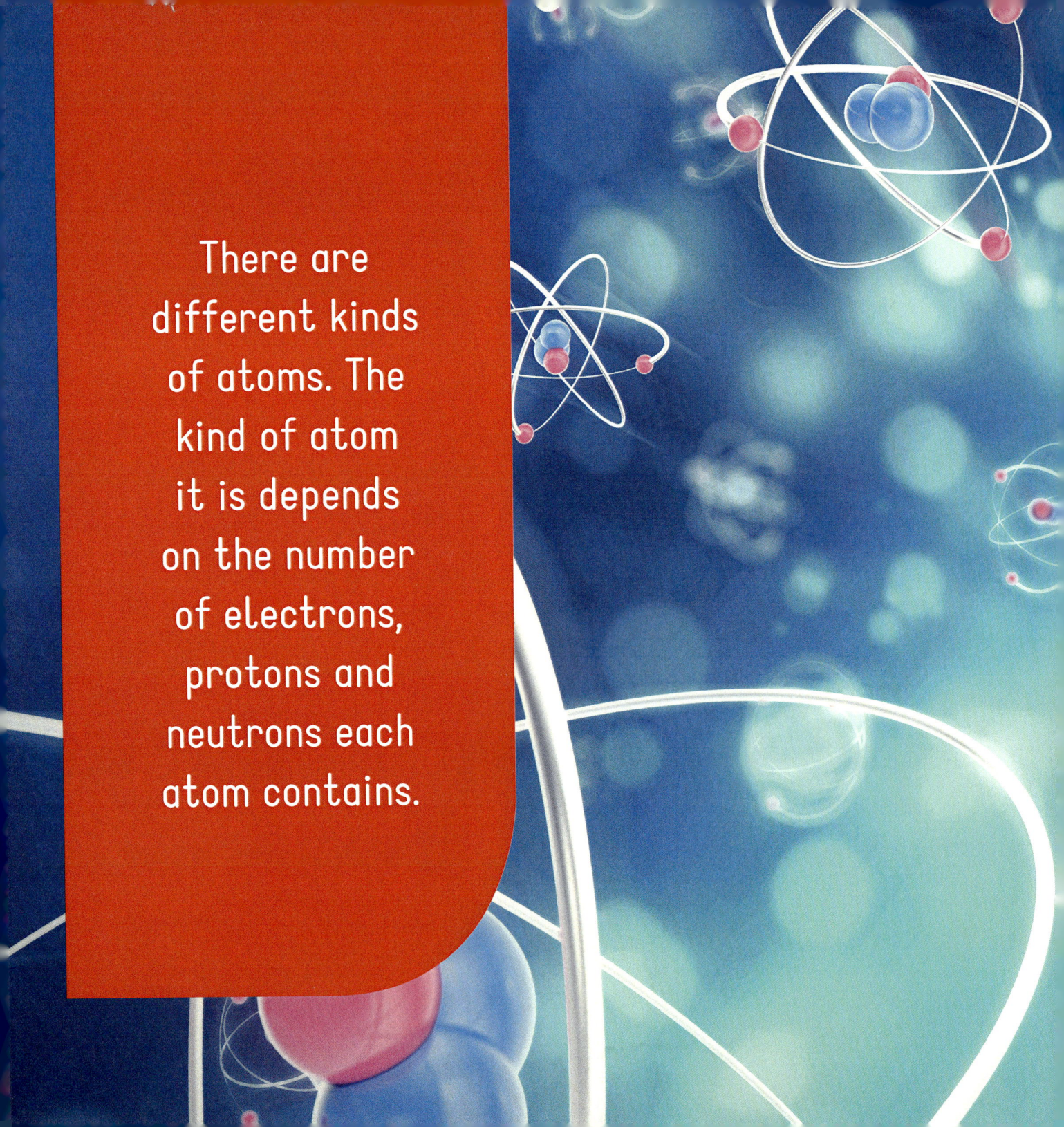

There are different kinds of atoms. The kind of atom it is depends on the number of electrons, protons and neutrons each atom contains.

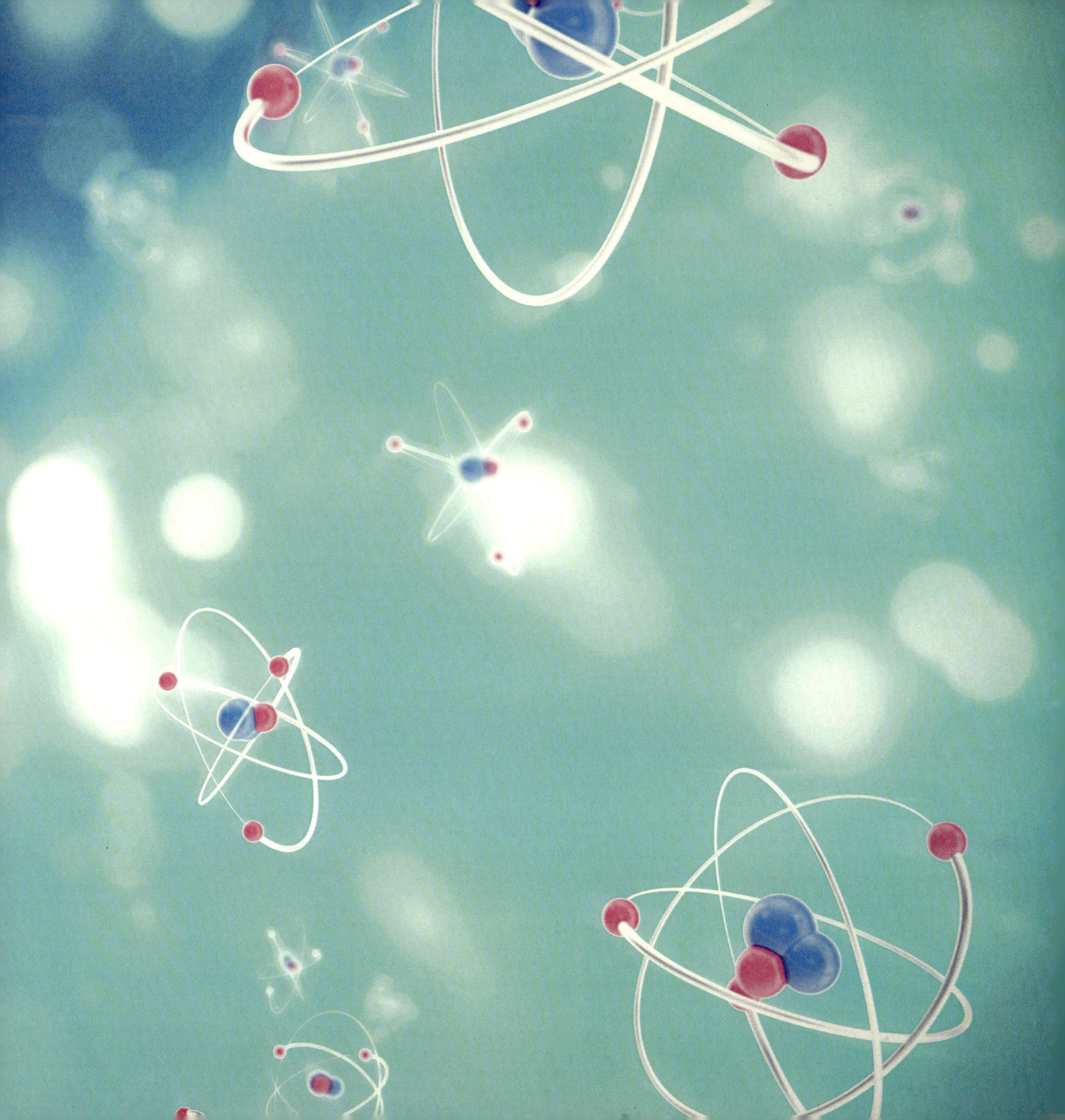

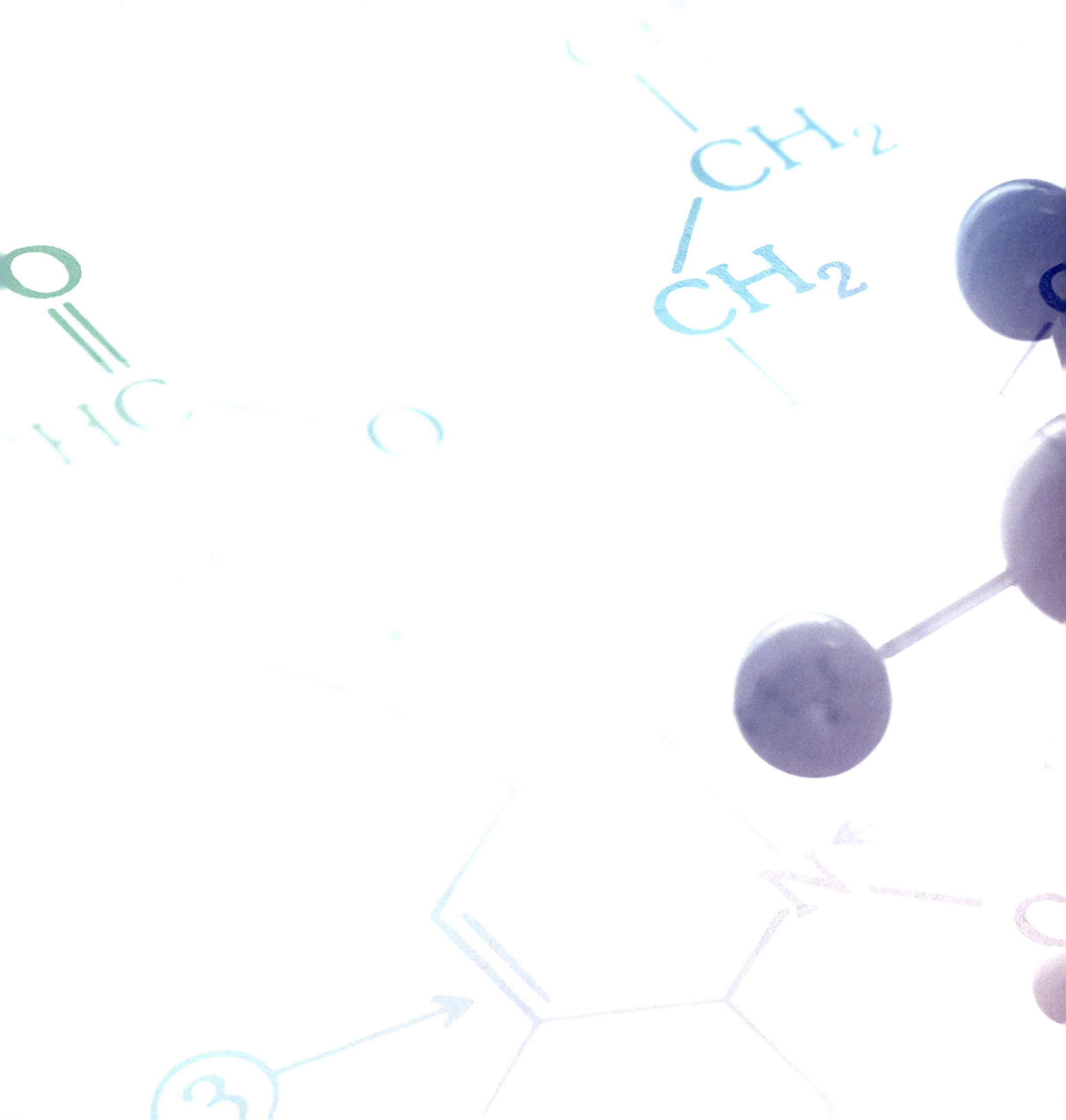
$CH_2$
$CH_2$

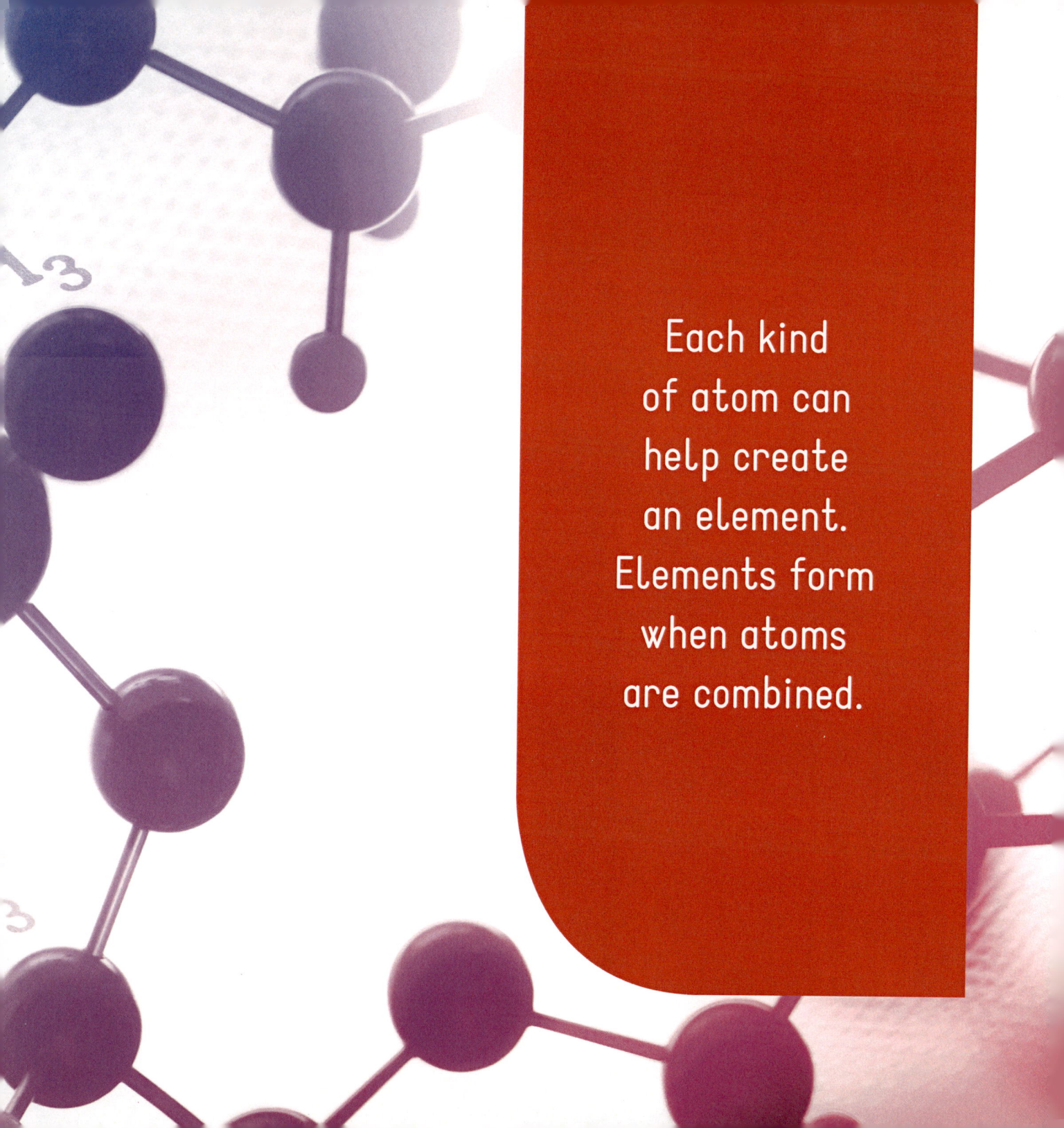

Each kind of atom can help create an element. Elements form when atoms are combined.

With the alphabet you can create a language; with elements of different kinds of atoms you can build a molecule (MOLL-uh-cyool). Molecules are groups of atoms joined together, the same way that words are groups of letters joined together.

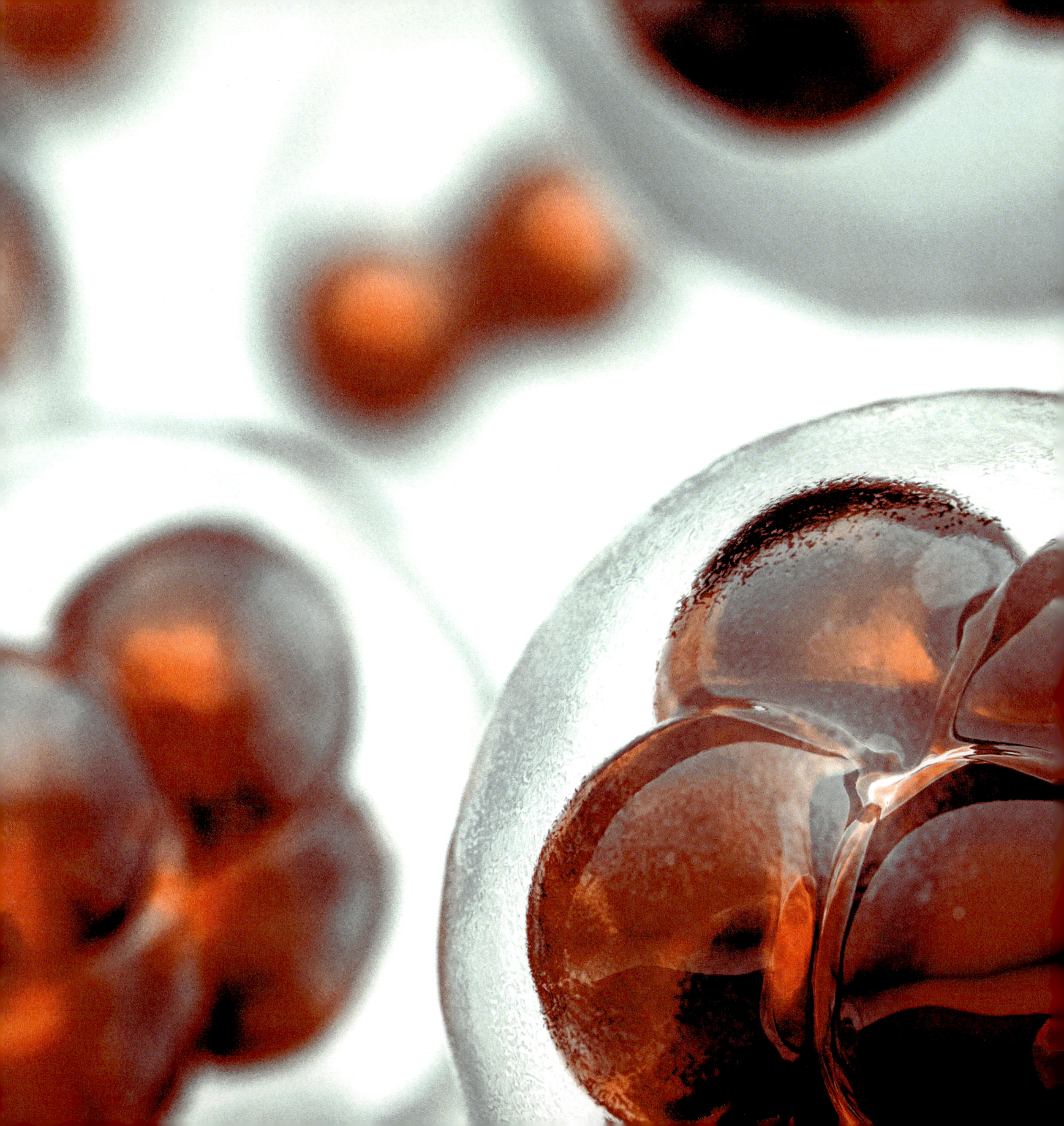

# MOLECULE

Like atoms, molecules are so small that nobody can see them. Molecules can only be seen in a special microscope.

Molecules can have different shapes. They can have short or long spirals while others may look like a pyramid. The shape of a molecule depends on the arrangement of bonds that hold its atoms together.

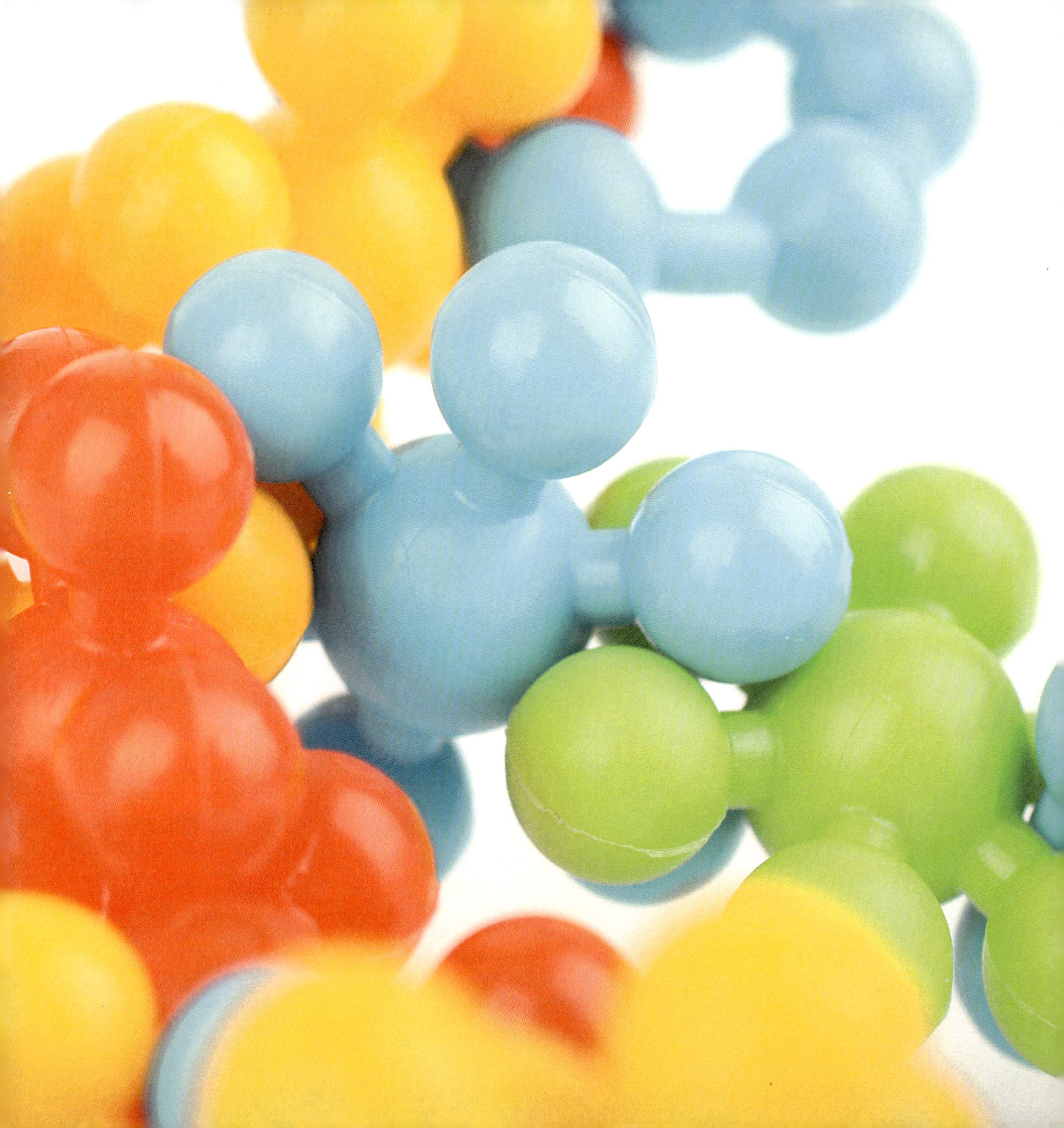

Hydrogen

Oxygen

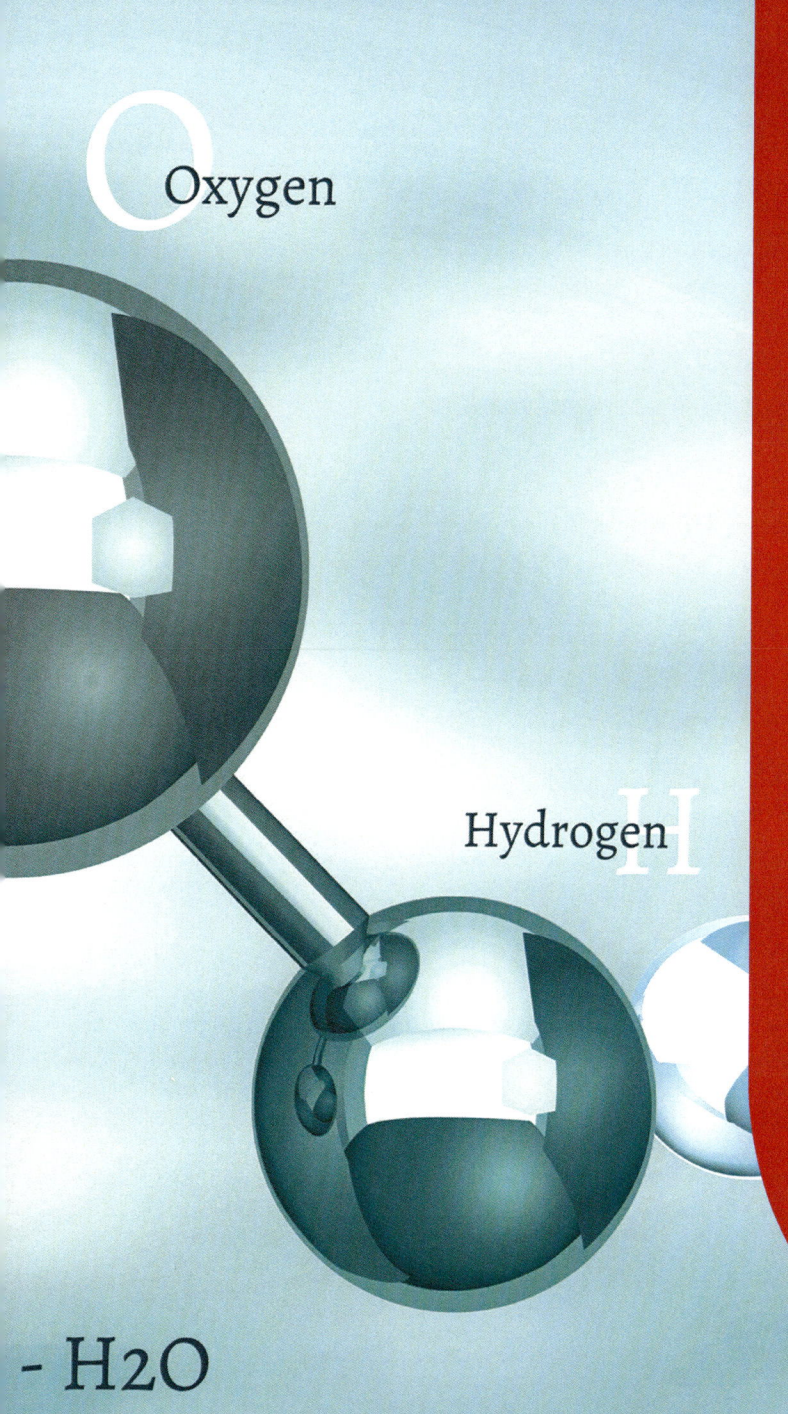

Hydrogen

- H2O

Molecules are not only made up of different types of atoms but also different ratios. For example the water molecule has 2 hydrogen atoms and 1 oxygen atom. It is written as H²O. Molecules can be simple or complicated.

For a molecule to survive, atoms have to stick together. This takes place when two atoms share electrons. Instead of spinning around one atom, the electron now spins around two. This process is called bonding.

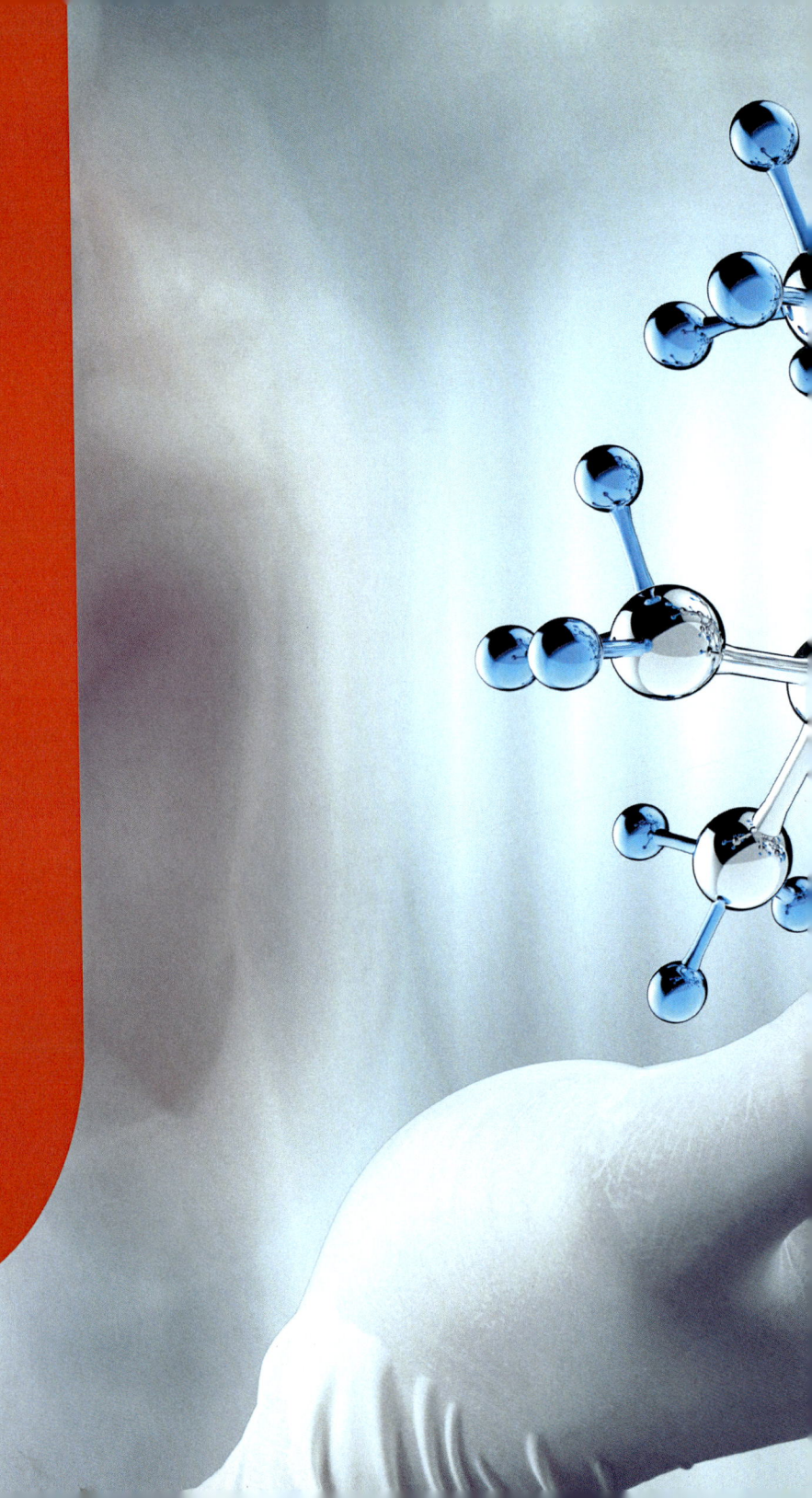

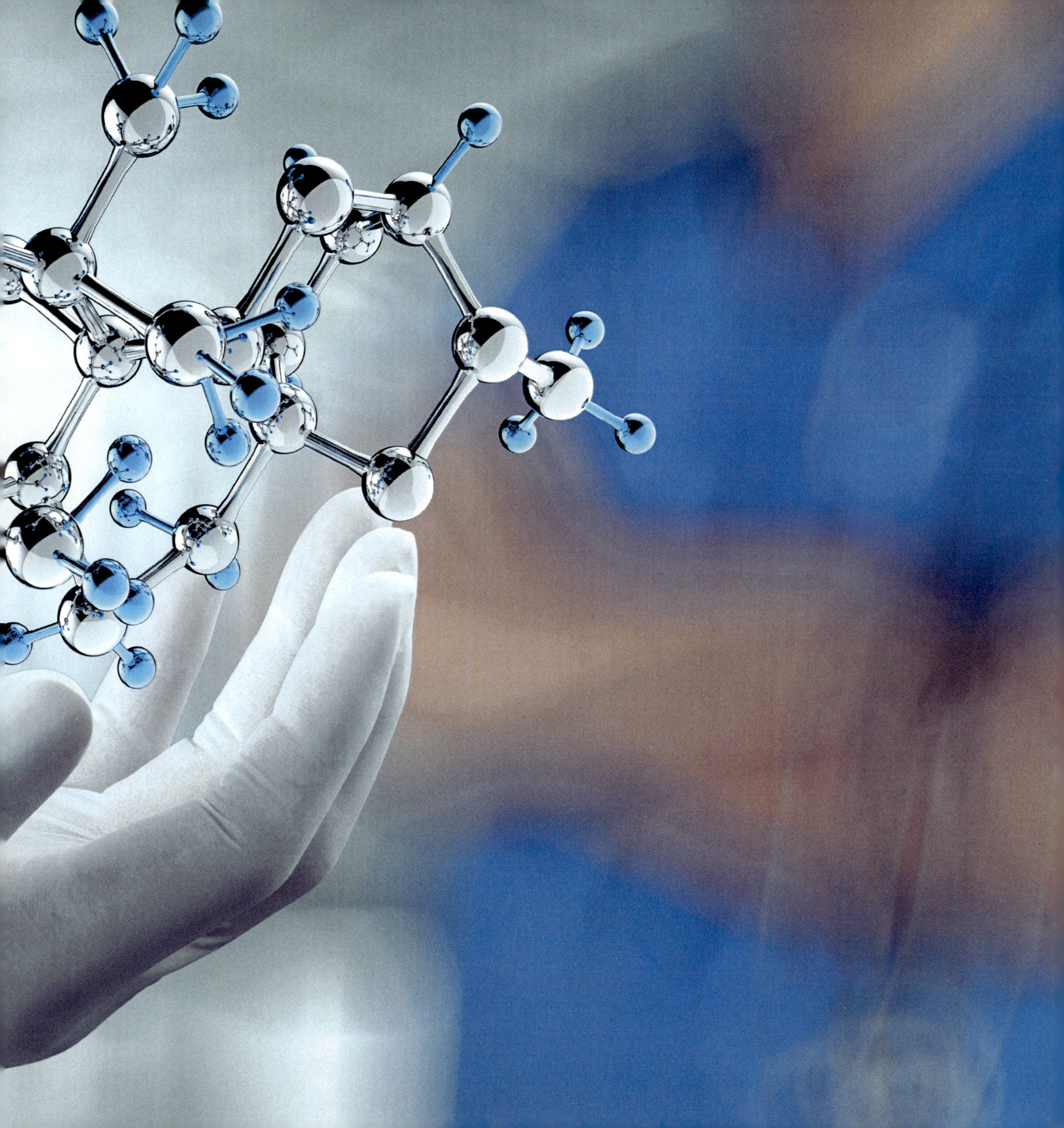

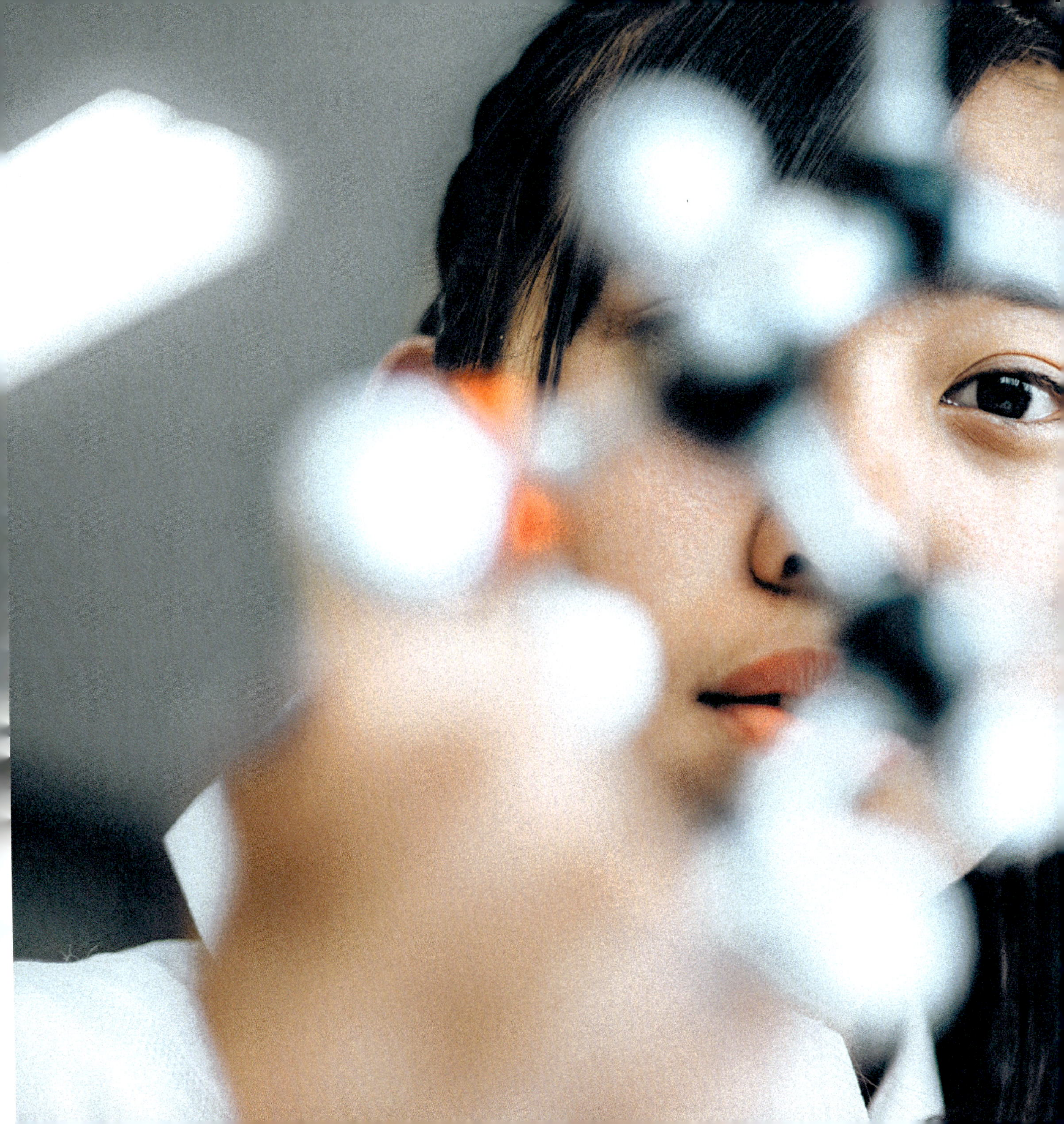

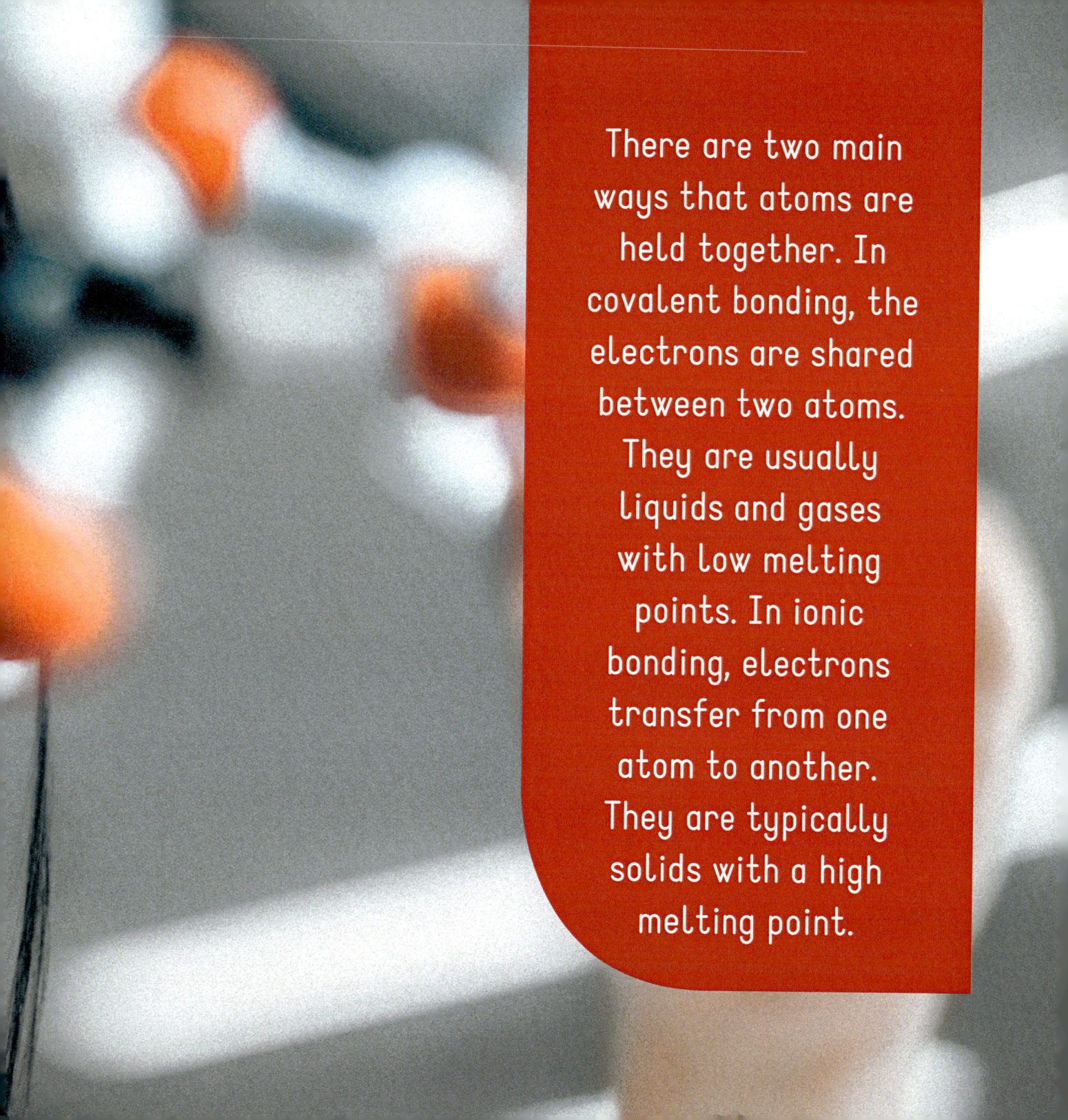

There are two main ways that atoms are held together. In covalent bonding, the electrons are shared between two atoms. They are usually liquids and gases with low melting points. In ionic bonding, electrons transfer from one atom to another. They are typically solids with a high melting point.

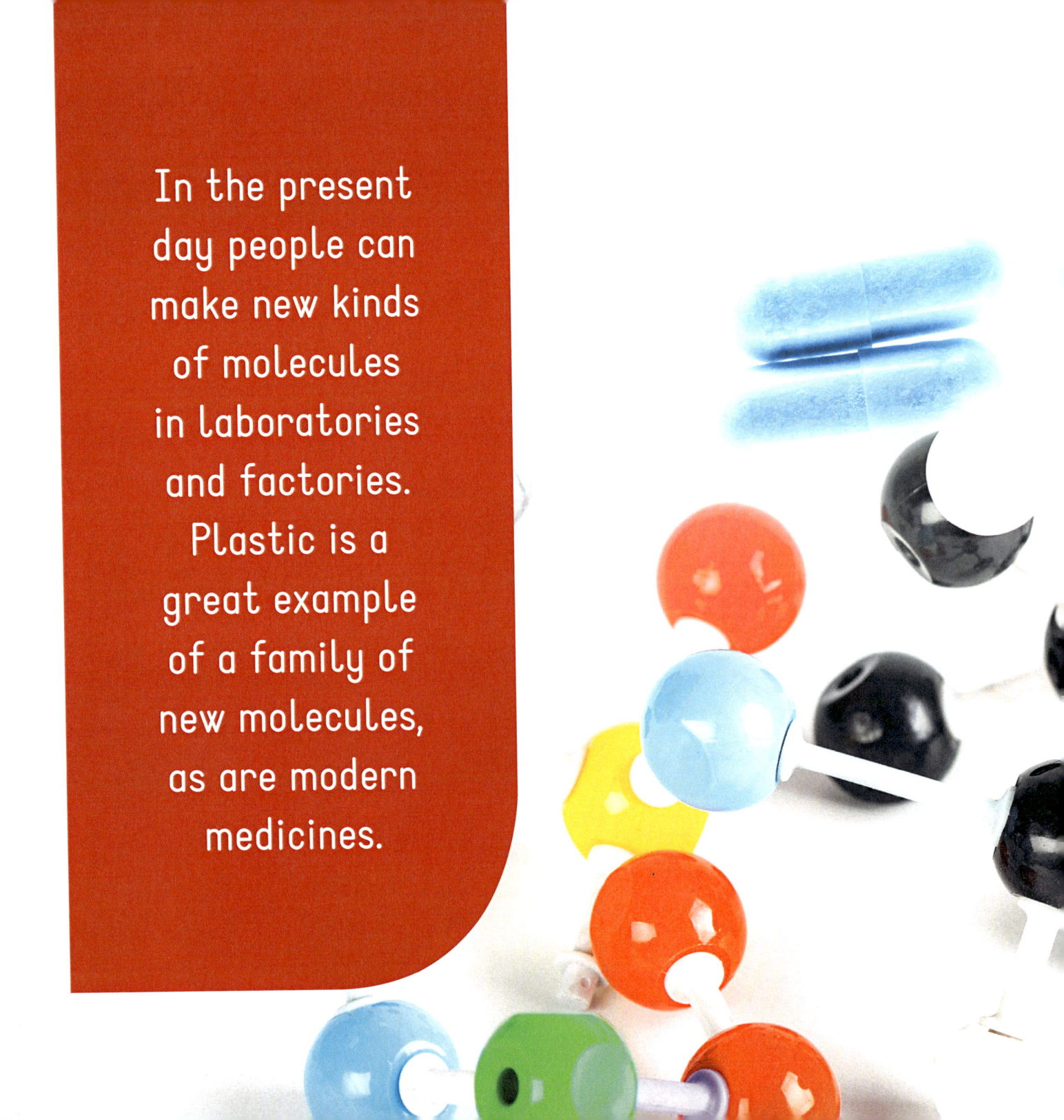

In the present day people can make new kinds of molecules in laboratories and factories. Plastic is a great example of a family of new molecules, as are modern medicines.

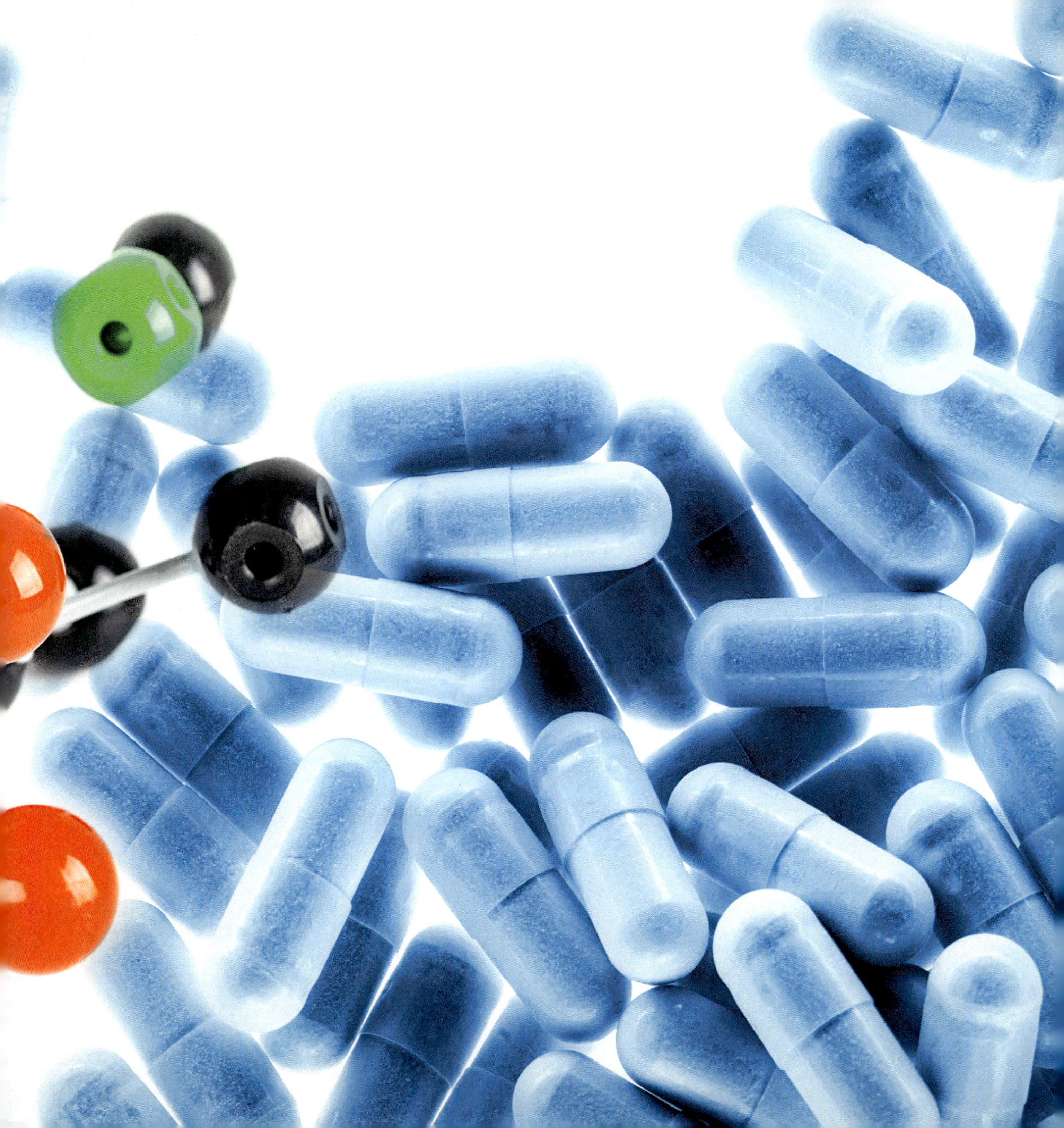

IA

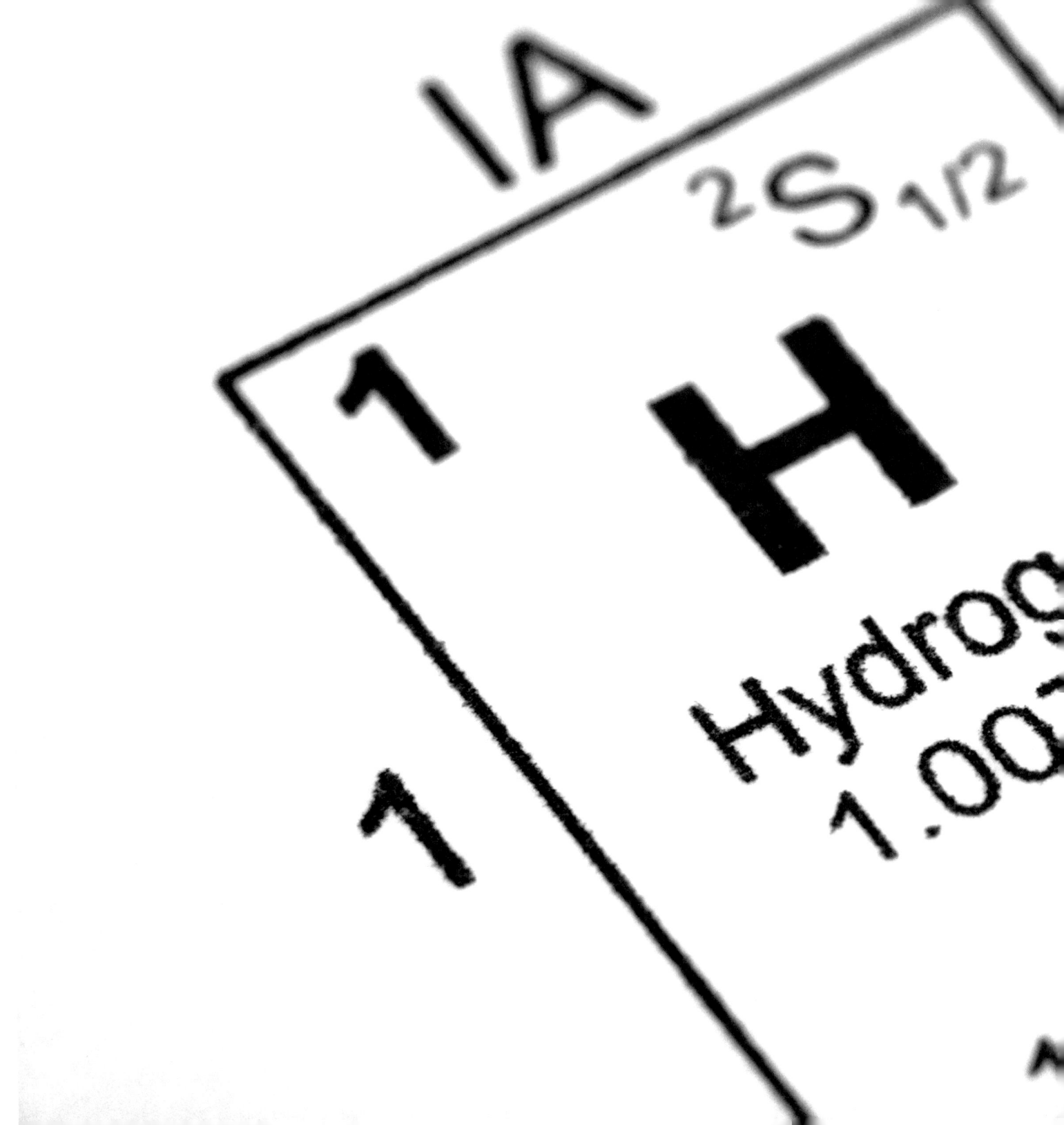

$^2S_{1/2}$

1

H

Hydrog
1.00

1

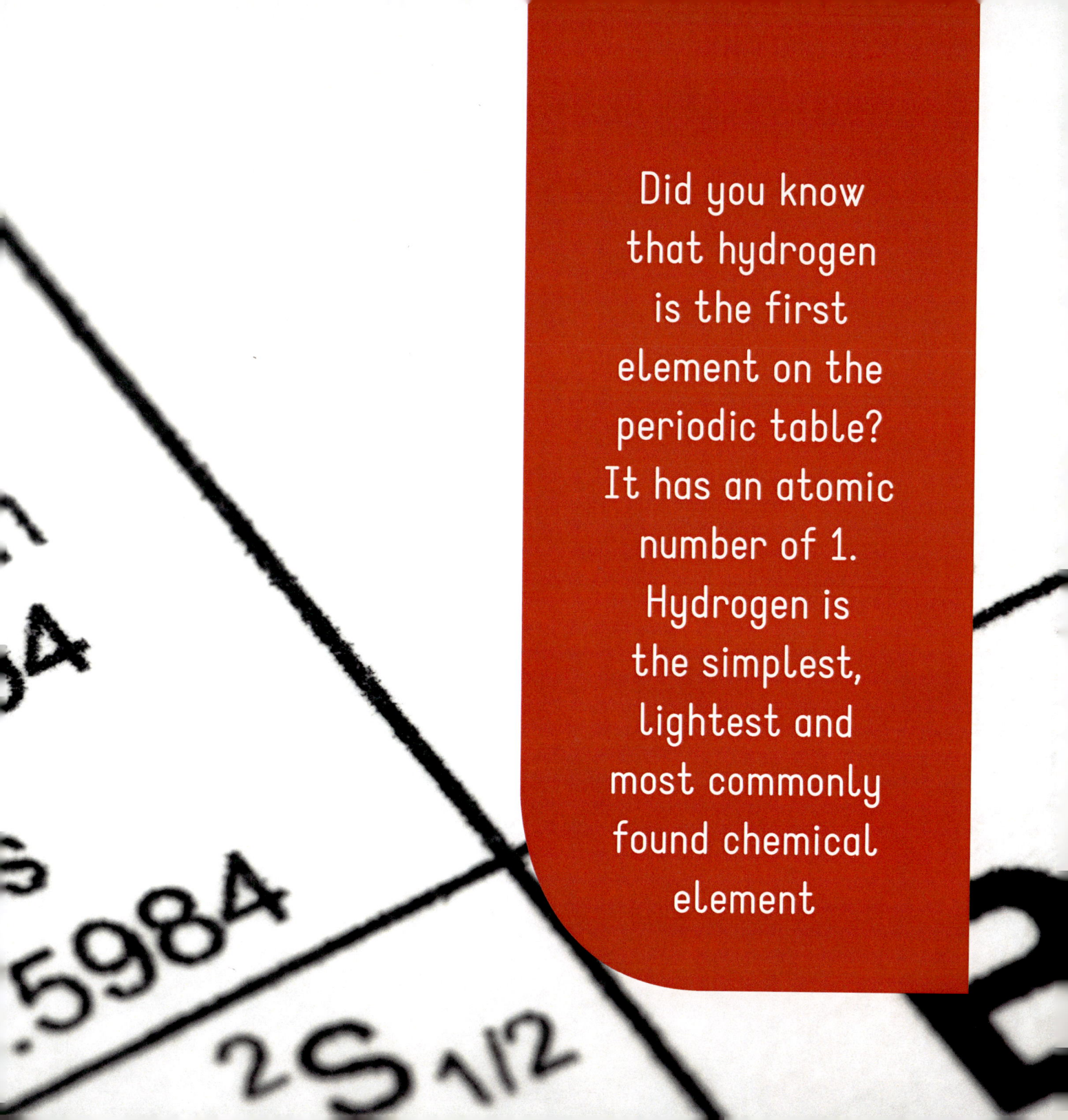

Did you know that hydrogen is the first element on the periodic table? It has an atomic number of 1. Hydrogen is the simplest, lightest and most commonly found chemical element

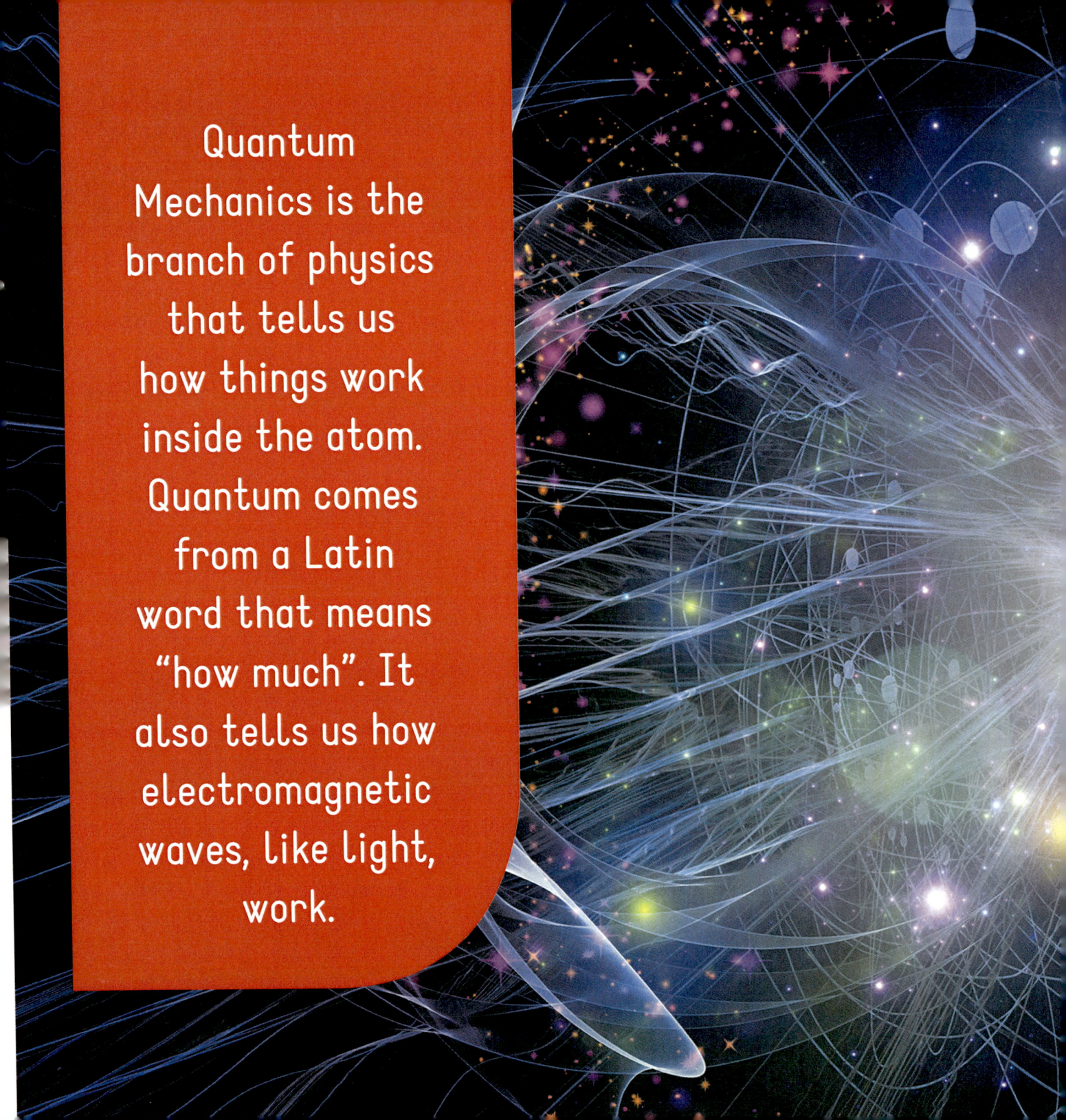

Quantum Mechanics is the branch of physics that tells us how things work inside the atom. Quantum comes from a Latin word that means "how much". It also tells us how electromagnetic waves, like light, work.

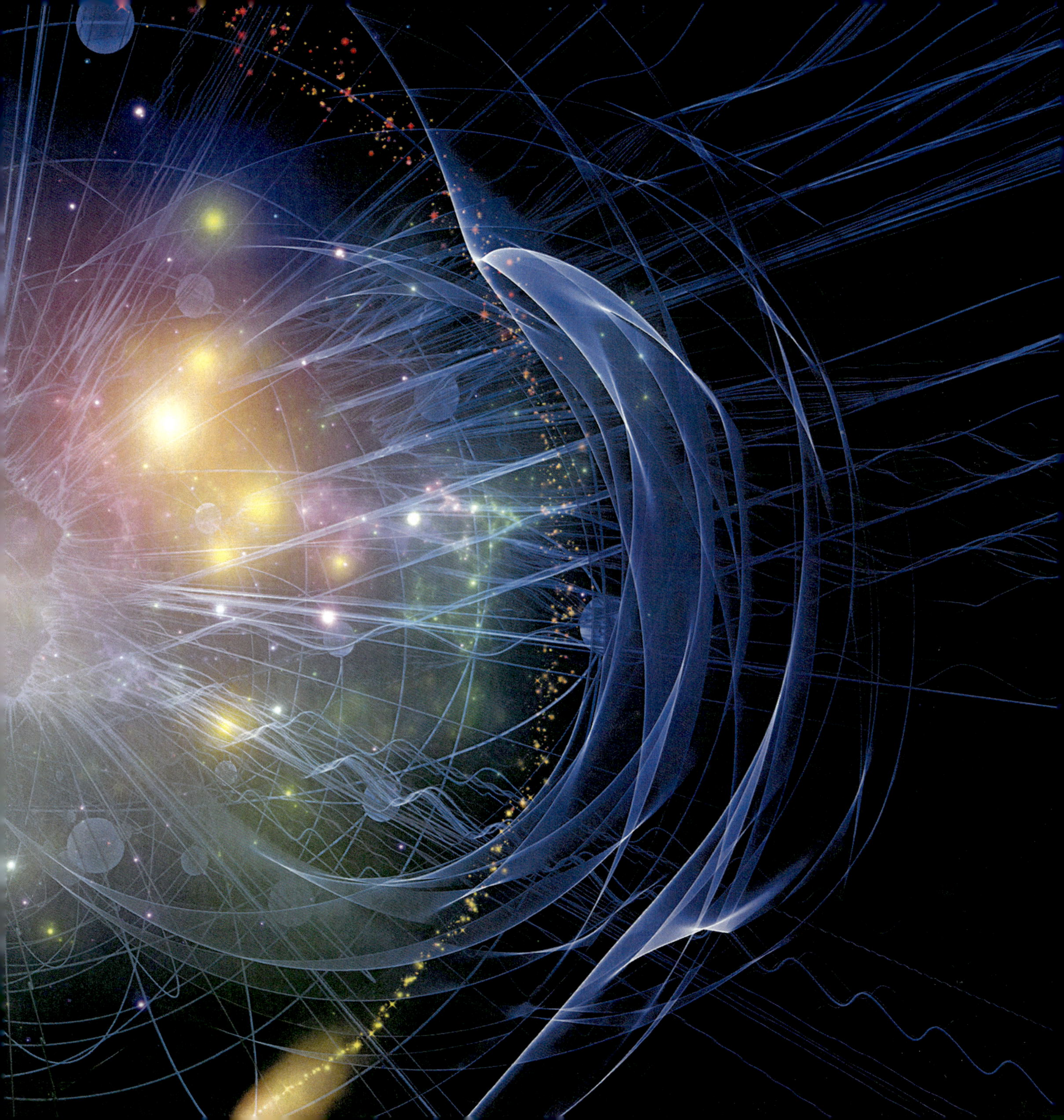

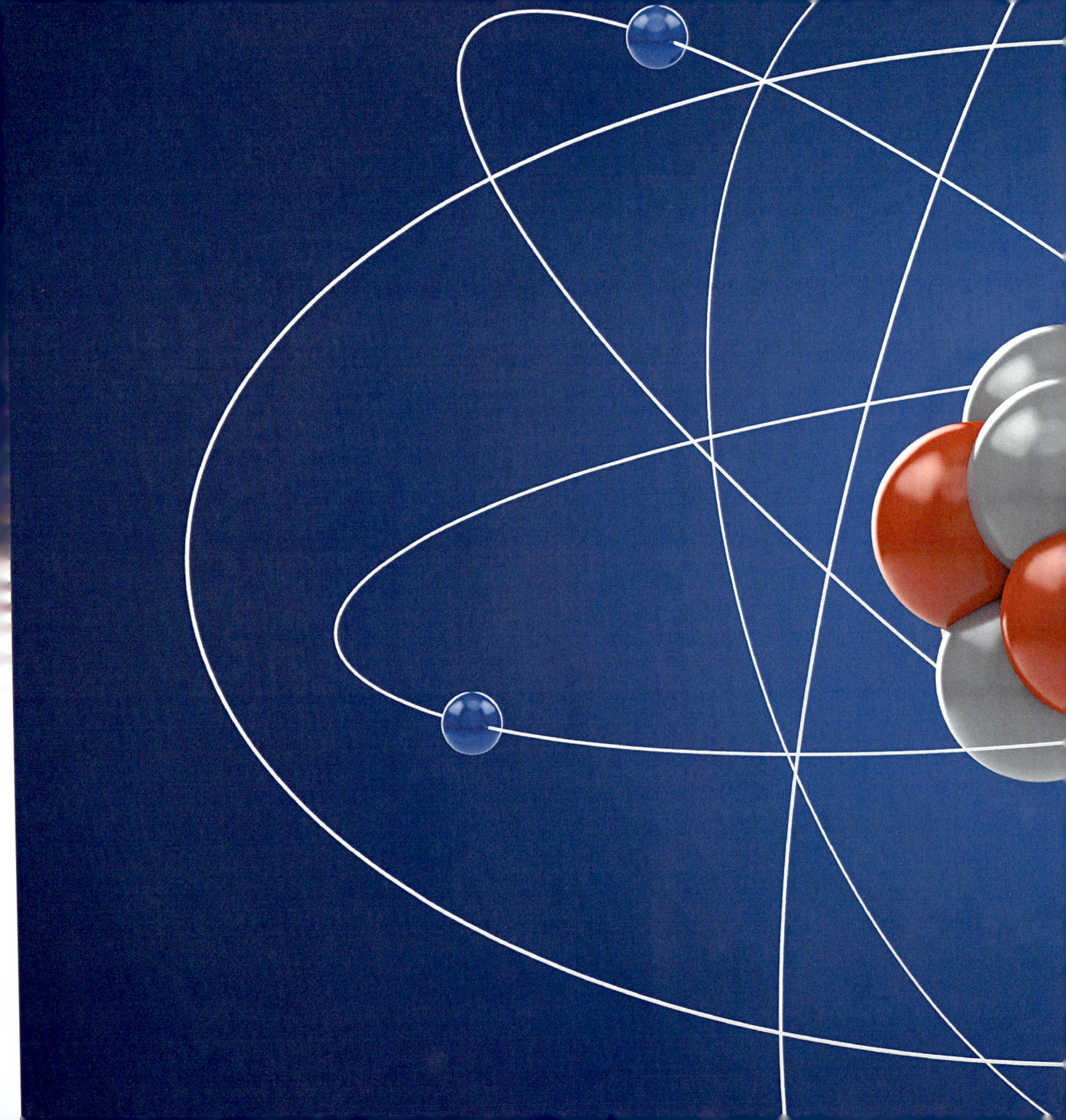

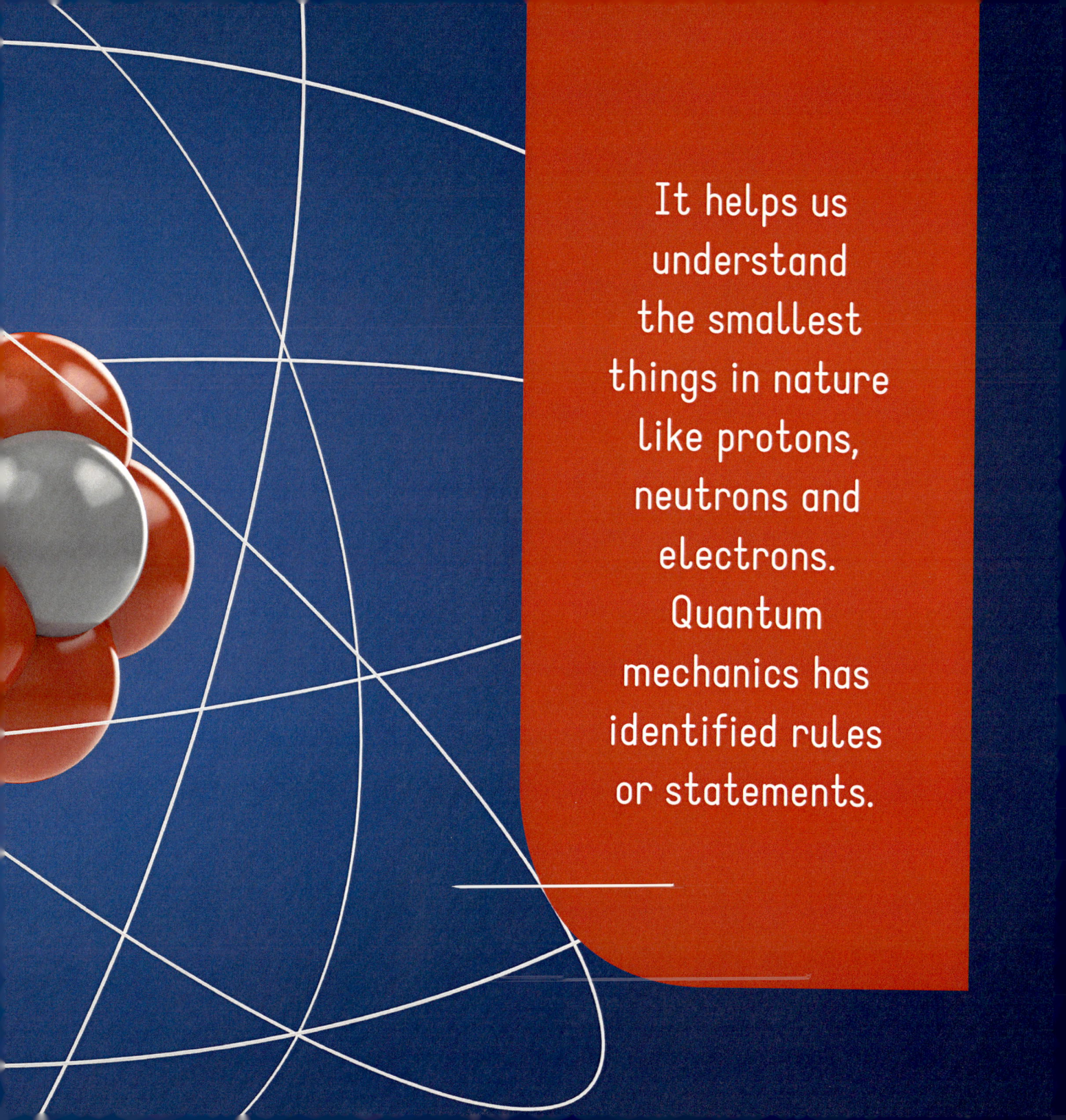

It helps us understand the smallest things in nature like protons, neutrons and electrons. Quantum mechanics has identified rules or statements.

It is based on observation about what kind of orbits electrons can have in an atom. The rules of quantum mechanics show what kinds of atoms can bind together.

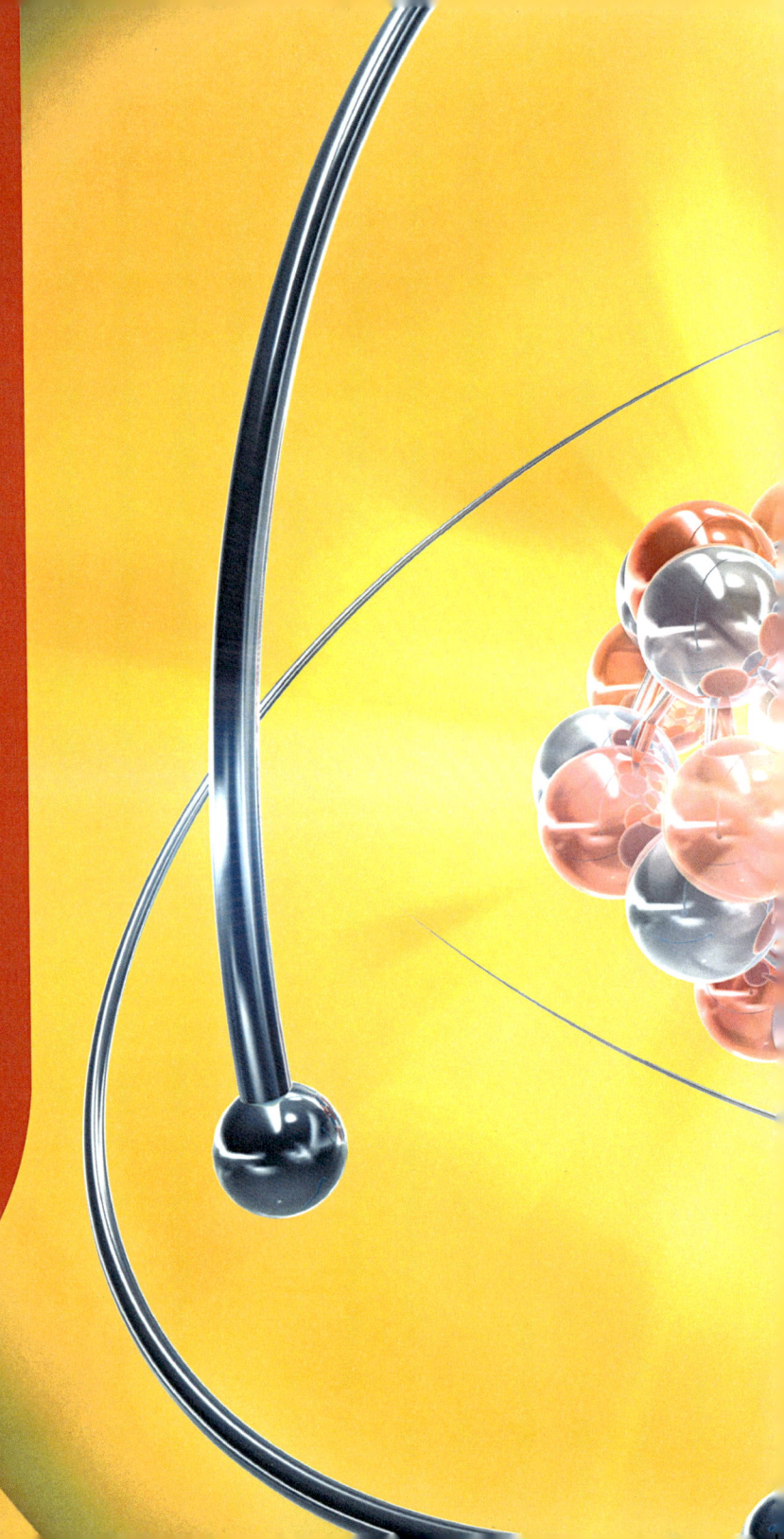

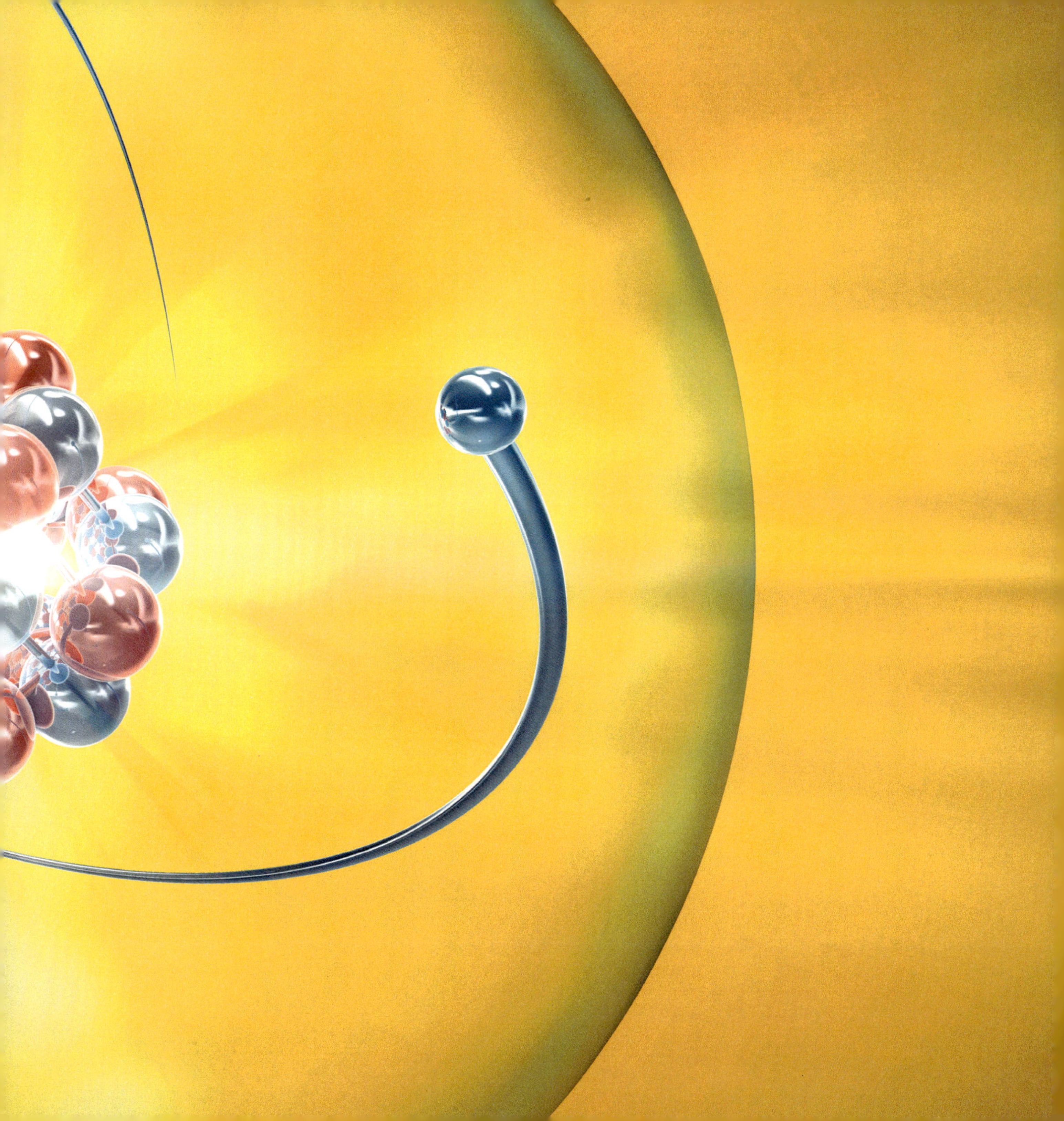

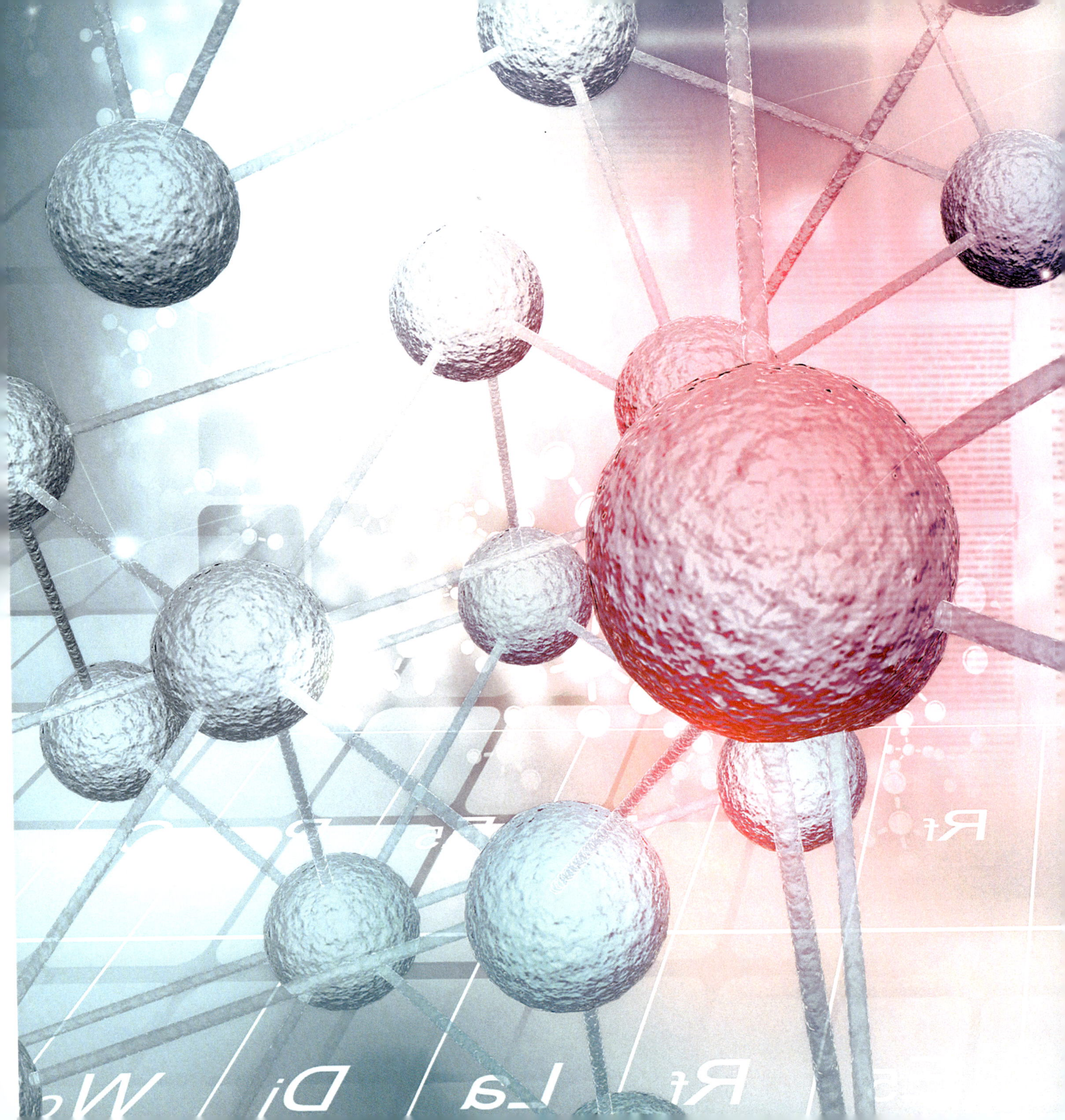

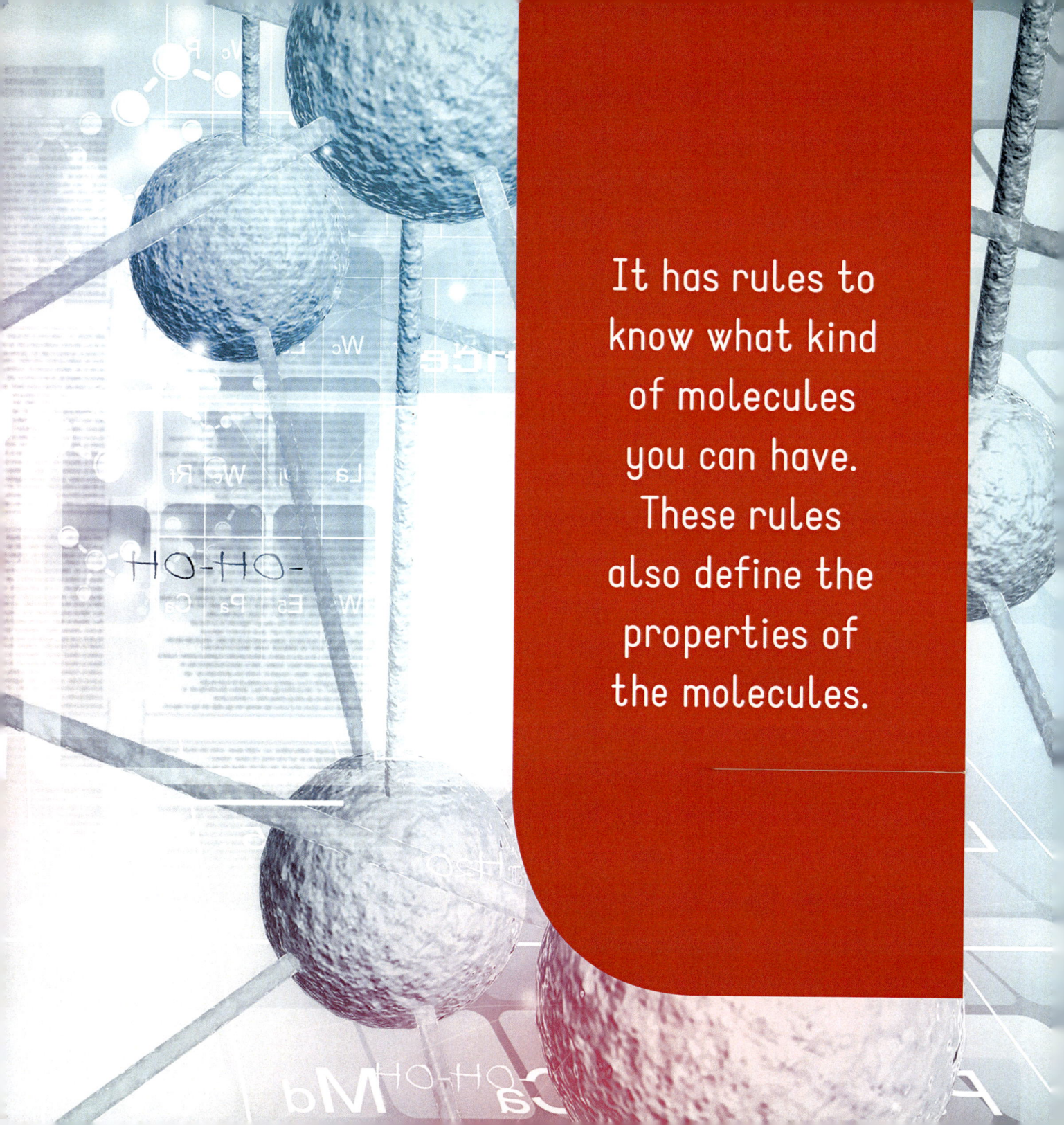

It has rules to know what kind of molecules you can have. These rules also define the properties of the molecules.

The most important parts of the rules of quantum mechanics cover how atoms bind together and how they interact with photons.

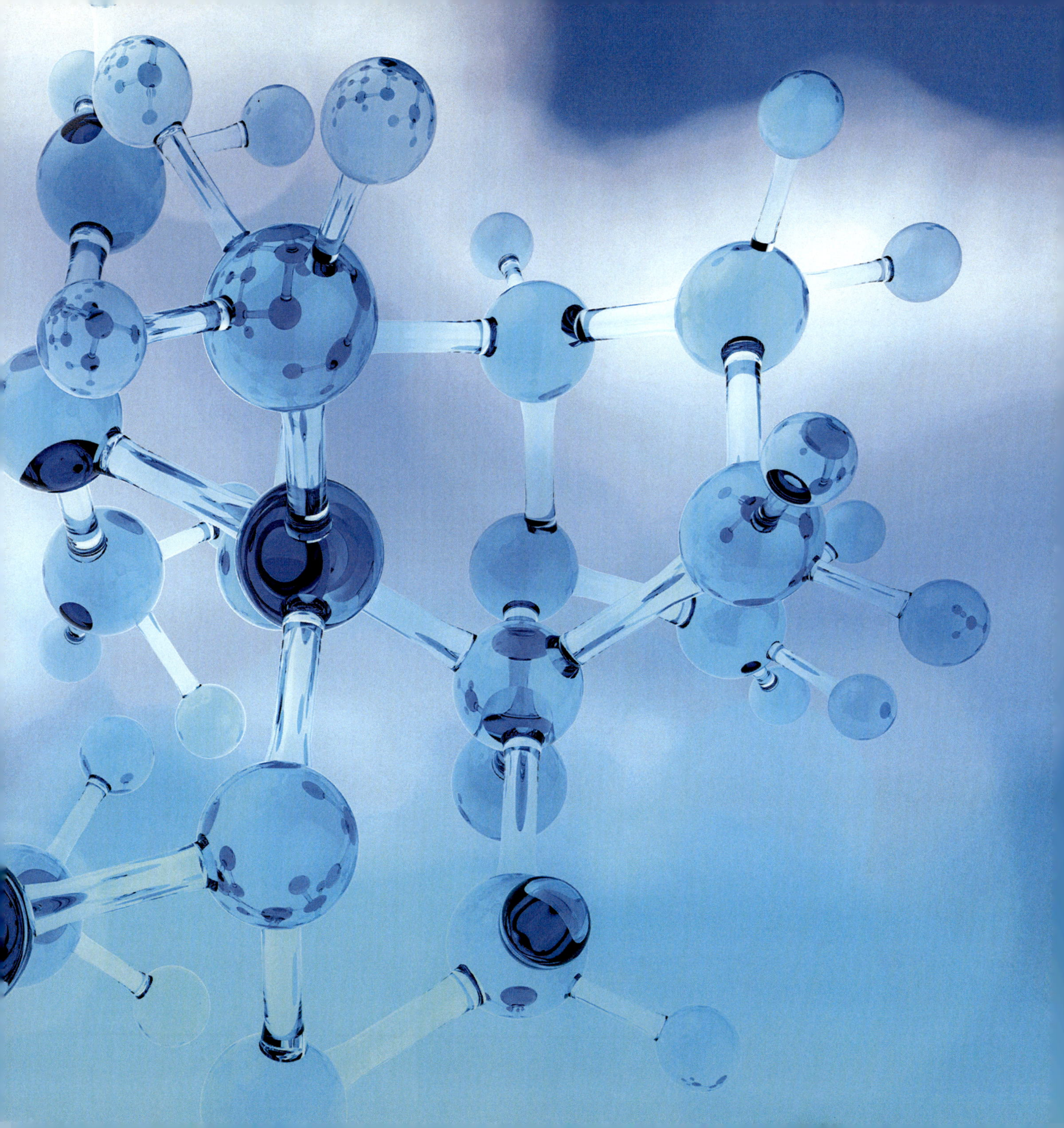

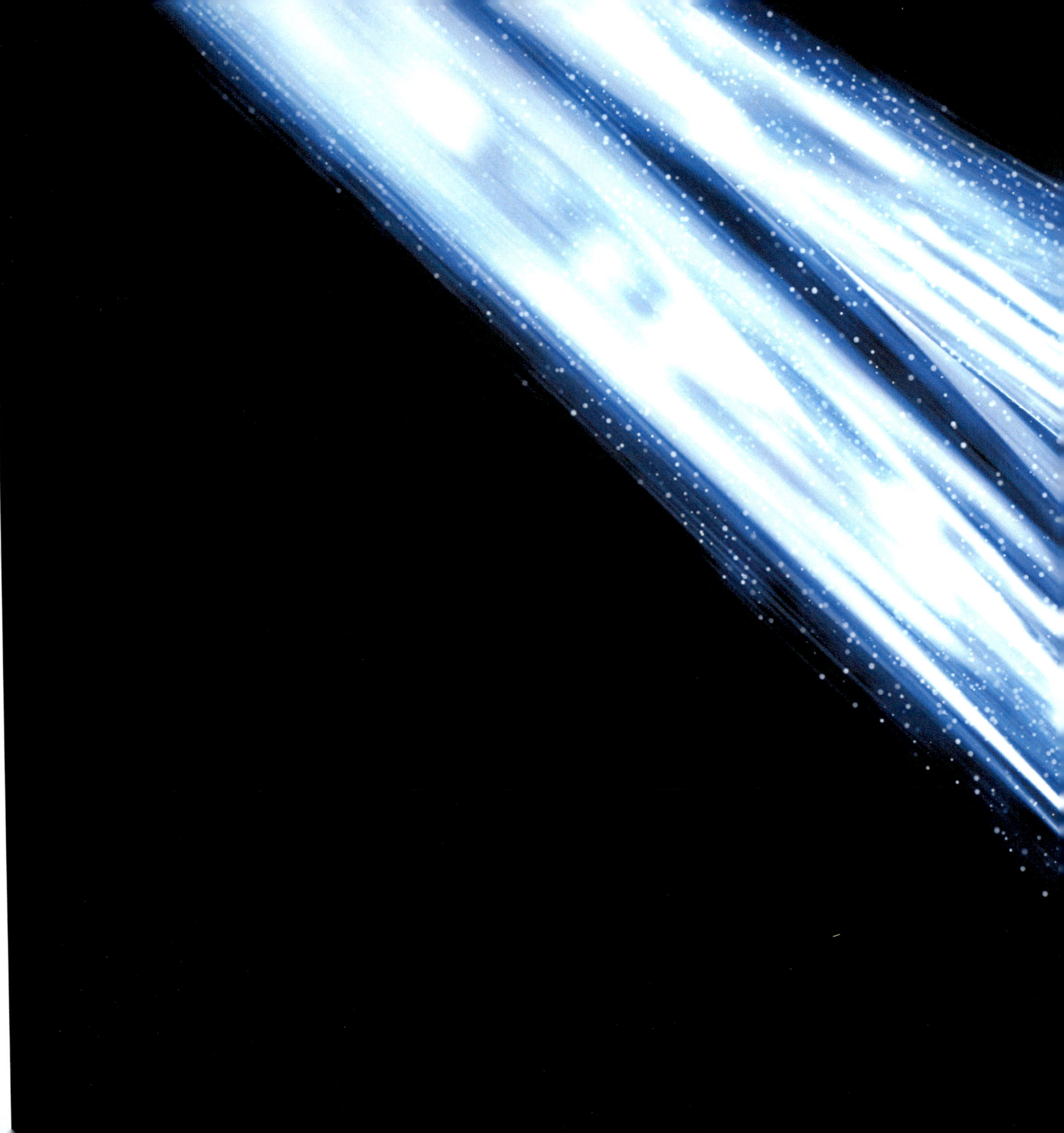

A photon is a pack of electromagnetic energy. It is the basic unit that creates light. The photon is known as a "quantum" of electromagnetic energy.

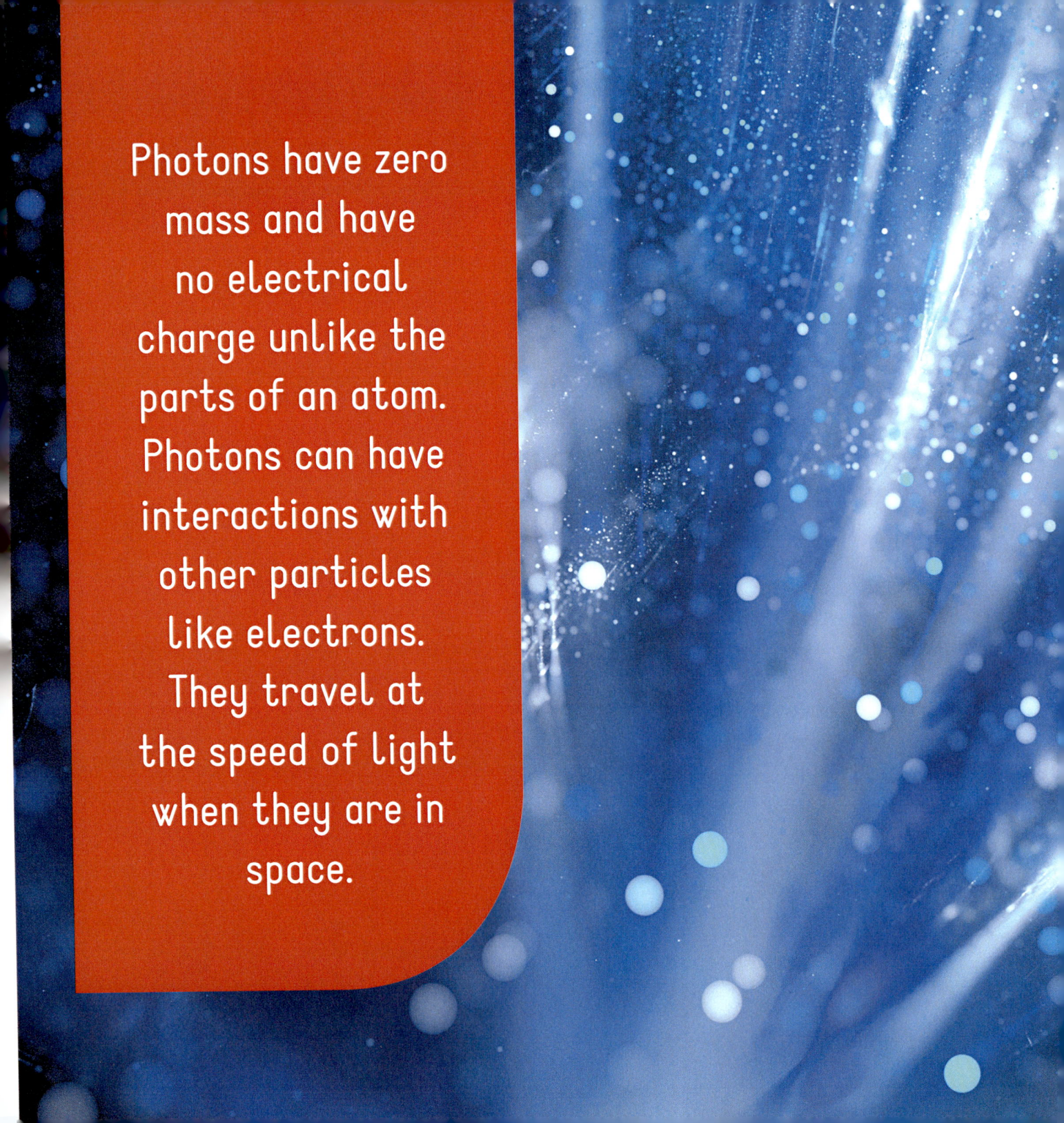

Photons have zero mass and have no electrical charge unlike the parts of an atom. Photons can have interactions with other particles like electrons. They travel at the speed of light when they are in space.

Physics is Fun!

Start studying things around you and discover new ideas.

Made in the USA
Middletown, DE
30 December 2017